Sacred Places

AMERICAN BIBLE SOCIETY

TIME HOME ENTERTAINMENT

PUBLISHER
Jim Childs

VICE PRESIDENT, BRAND & DIGITAL STRATEGY
Steven Sandonato

EXECUTIVE DIRECTOR, MARKETING SERVICES
Carol Pittard

EXECUTIVE DIRECTOR, RETAIL & SPECIAL SALES
Tom Mifsud

EXECUTIVE PUBLISHING DIRECTOR
Joy Butts

DIRECTOR, BOOKAZINE DEVELOPMENT & MARKETING
Laura Adam

FINANCE DIRECTOR
Glenn Buonocore

ASSOCIATE PUBLISHING DIRECTOR
Megan Pearlman

ASSOCIATE GENERAL COUNSEL
Helen Wan

ASSISTANT DIRECTOR, SPECIAL SALES
Ilene Schreider

BRAND MANAGER, PRODUCT MARKETING
Nina Fleishman Reed

ASSOCIATE PRODUCTION MANAGER
Kimberly Marshall

ASSOCIATE PREPRESS MANAGER
Alex Voznesenskiy

EDITORIAL DIRECTOR
Stephen Koepp

COPY CHIEF
Rina Bander

DESIGN MANAGER
Anne-Michelle Gallero

GENERAL EDITOR
Christopher D. Hudson

SENIOR EDITOR
Ben Irwin

CONSULTING EDITORS
Philip H. Towner, Ph.D.
Barbara Bernstengel, M.A.
Robert Hodgson, Ph.D.
Davina McDonald, M.A.
Thomas R. May, M.Div.
With special thanks to the American Bible Society's Committee
on Translation and Scholarship

WRITERS
Randy Southern
Christopher D. Hudson
Selena Sarns

DESIGN AND PRODUCTION
Mark Wainwright, Symbology Creative

SPECIAL THANKS: Katherine Barnet, Jeremy Biloon, Susan
Chodakiewicz, Rose Cirrincione, Jacqueline Fitzgerald, Christine
Font, Jenna Goldberg, Hillary Hirsch, David Kahn, Mona Li,
Amy Mangus, Nina Mistry, Dave Rozzelle, Ricardo Santiago,
Adriana Tierno, Vanessa Wu

Unless otherwise noted, all Scripture quotations are from the *Holy Bible,
Contemporary English Version* (CEV). Copyright 2006 by the American Bible Society.
Used by permission of the American Bible Society. All rights reserved.

ISBN 10: **1-61893-067-2**
ISBN 13: **978-1-61893-067-5**
Library of Congress Control Number: **2013945253**

We welcome your comments and suggestions about Time Home Entertainment Books.
Please write to us at:

Time Home Entertainment Books
Attention: Book Editors
PO Box 11016
Des Moines, IA 50336-1016

If you would like to order any of our hardcover Collector's Edition books,
please call us at 1-800-327-6388, Monday through Friday, 7 a.m. to 8 p.m.,
or Saturday, 7 a.m. to 6 p.m., Central Time.

ART SOURCES

Shutterstock
Photos marked BiblePlaces.com are used with permission.
Thinkstock
iStock
TheBIblePeople.com

Table of Contents

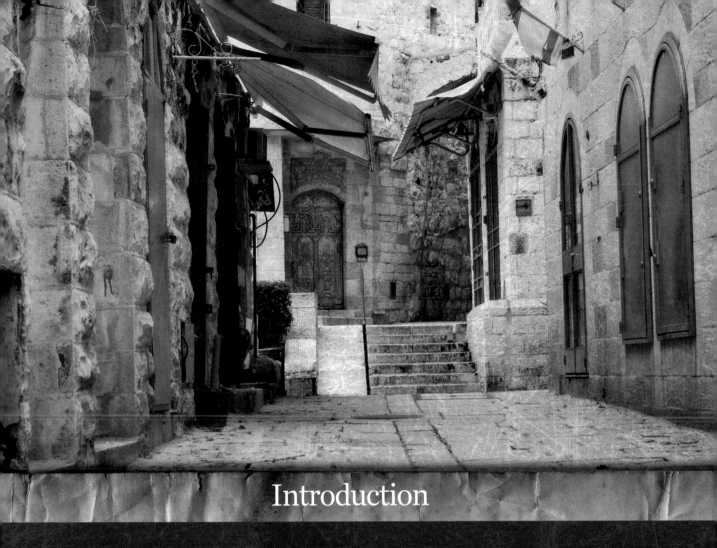

Introduction

The stories of the Bible are steeped in a strong sense of *place*. The Bible is not composed of ethereal, disembodied thoughts. It has a real-world context; its drama is set in both ordinary and extraordinary earthly locations. Place matters immensely when reading the Bible.

The Old Testament depicts God carving out spaces on earth where he can dwell with people. The first is a garden, surrounded by some of the most famous rivers in ancient Mesopotamia. Later, God promises an elderly nomad named Abraham an inheritance situated between Mesopotamia and Egypt. This "promised land" becomes the kingdom of Israel and is the setting for much of the biblical narrative. As the story progresses, the fortunes of God's people are often tied to this small patch of earth.

The concept of place is no less important as we enter the New Testament. The good news about Jesus takes root against the backdrop of the Roman Empire and spreads into the major urban centers of Asia Minor (modern-day Turkey), Greece, and Rome itself.

Many sacred places of the Bible have been lost to history; they have become the stuff of speculation and archaeological expedition. Many others are known to us today. The ancient Israelites had a habit of marking sacred places—sometimes with crude stones, sometimes with elaborate monuments. As the Church has spread across the world, Christians have continued this practice right down to modern times. These markers serve as signposts of our spiritual

Introduction

In the beginning, there was Mesopotamia. At least, that's what our best archaeological evidence suggests. (The precise locations for some biblical sites, however, have yet to be determined.) When life on the earth was first created, God chose as ground zero a fertile patch of land in what many believe is now Iraq, northeastern Syria, southeastern Turkey, and southwestern Iran.

It is believed that certain biblical sites, such as Babylon, Ur, and Haran were all located in Mesopotamia and may have been home to Adam and Eve, Noah, and (for the first part of his life) Abram, the patriarch of the Jewish people. Any exploration of sacred places in the Bible has to begin here.

Mesopotamia

Life in Mesopotamia—if indeed this was the location of the famed Garden of Eden—started well enough. In this idyllic setting, Adam and Eve tended to the garden and its inhabitants, gave names to the animals, walked with God in the cool of the evening, and enjoyed his creation. Unfortunately, the good times last all of twenty-two verses in the Genesis narrative (2:4–25). The tide turns the moment Adam and Eve taste the forbidden fruit—at which point life as they knew it in Eden came to an end.

At this point, the story narrows its focus on one man and his family. God instructs Abram, a man from Ur who trusted in and obeyed God, to leave Mesopotamia (by way of Haran) and journey to a new land—a place called Canaan, which Abram's descendants would someday call their own.

above: The ancient town of Hasankeyf, Turkey

The Garden of Eden

GENESIS 1–3

The location of the Garden of Eden—the place the biblical account suggests where humankind began—is one of the enduring mysteries of the Bible. The book of Genesis offers a few tantalizing clues. Genesis 2:14 identifies the Euphrates as one of four rivers that flowed through Eden.

Today the Euphrates River flows from eastern Turkey, through Syria and then Iraq, where it converges with the Tigris River and empties into the Persian Gulf. Many scholars point to the area on the northwest shores of the Persian Gulf as a potential site for the Garden of Eden. Others suggest a location in upper Mesopotamia—near the modern-day city of Batman, Turkey, just west of Lake Van.

The word *Eden* may derive from the Hebrew word for pleasure or delight—or possibly from the Mesopotamian word for a plain. The description of the garden in Genesis 2 suggests an idyllic setting, capable of sustaining a staggering array of animal and plant life.

The loss of Eden—and the banishment of Adam and Eve from the garden—ranks as the most devastating event in human history. Banished from paradise, Adam and Eve (and later their descendants) were forced to make their home in the less hospitable lands of Mesopotamia.

THE GARDEN OF EDEN IN THE BIBLE

From Eden a river flowed out to water the garden, then it divided into four rivers. The first one is the Pishon River that flows through the land of Havilah, where pure gold, rare perfumes, and precious stones are found. The second is the Gihon River that winds through Ethiopia. The Tigris River that flows east of Assyria is the third, and the fourth is the Euphrates River. (Genesis 2:10–14)

The Euphrates River played an important role in Old Testament geography, even after Adam and Eve were sent out from the Garden of Eden. Typically, the river served as a reference point. In Genesis 15:18 God made this promise to Abraham: *"I will give your descendants the land east of the Shihor River on the border of Egypt as far as the Euphrates River."* First Kings 4:21 describes the extent of Solomon's reign by pointing out that he *"ruled every kingdom between the Euphrates River and the land of the Philistines down to Egypt."*

background image: The Euphrates River

The Ararat Mountains

GENESIS 6–8

The sinful tendencies that led to Adam and Eve's expulsion from the Garden of Eden also ran rampant through their children and their children's children. When the level of wickedness and corruption reached a tipping point, God intervened, sending a flood that covered the earth and killed everything that drew breath—with the exception of Noah, his family, and the animals they gathered onto their ark.

The Bible does not tell us where Noah was born or where he lived before the flood, but it does tell us where he wound up. For 150 days, the ark drifted as floodwaters filled—and then receded from—the earth. And then the giant lifeboat came to rest. Specifically, the ark ran aground on the mountains of Ararat, which are located in modern-day Turkey. The mountain chain has two primary peaks: Greater Ararat, with an elevation of nearly 17,000 feet, and Lesser Ararat, with an elevation of almost 13,000 feet. Many scholars believe the ark came to rest on one of these two peaks. The Bible, however, does not specify.

Some explorers claim to have spotted remnants of the ark on the slopes of Ararat. No one, however, has offered definitive proof of the ark's resting place.

ARARAT IN THE BIBLE

Then on the seventeenth day of the seventh month of the year, the boat came to rest somewhere in the Ararat mountains. (Genesis 8:4)

After Noah emptied the ark, he built an altar to worship God. Pleased by Noah's faithfulness, God made a solemn covenant with him, vowing never to destroy the earth with water again. But that's not all.

"God said to Noah and his sons: 'I am giving you my blessing. Have a lot of children and grandchildren, so people will live everywhere on this earth' " (Genesis 9:1). God intended the mountains of Ararat to be humanity's second great starting point. He expected a post-flood migration from Ararat to every corner of the globe.

Chapter 10 in Genesis describes how the descendants of Noah's sons populated the known world.

The mountains of Ararat

MOUNT ARARAT?

■ *In 2 Kings 19:37, Ararat is identified as the place where the sons of the Assyrian King Sennacherib fled after killing their father.*

Babylon

GENESIS 11

Babylonia was a kingdom in southern Mesopotamia, situated between the Tigris and Euphrates Rivers, in what is now southern Iraq. The capital city, Babylon, was located about fifty miles north of modern-day Baghdad. The Hebrew name for Babylon is Babel.

After the flood, many of Noah's descendants settled in the plain of Babylon. They shared a common language—and an uncommon ambition. They wanted to make a name for themselves by creating a tower that would reach heaven. Some scholars believe the tower was a ziggurat, a stepped temple with a rectangular or square base.

God thwarted their ambition by confusing their speech—causing different groups of people to speak different languages. Communication became virtually impossible, so the tower of Babel was abandoned.

BABYLON IN THE BIBLE

At first everyone spoke the same language, but after some of them moved from the east and settled in Babylonia, they said: "Let's build a city with a tower that reaches to the sky! We'll use hard bricks and tar instead of stone and mortar. We'll become famous, and we won't be scattered all over the world." (Genesis 11:1–4)

■ *The tower of Babel marks the first time in the biblical narrative that this region (and city) is cast in a negative light—but it would not be the last. Few names are as reliably villainous in Scripture as Babylon. In 586 BC, under King Nebuchadnezzar, the Babylonians destroyed Jerusalem and the temple, the center of Jewish worship. Babylon also figures symbolically in the apostle John's apocalyptic visions in the book of Revelation (Revelation 14:8).*

The fallout from the tower of Babel led to the fulfillment of God's instructions in Genesis 1. *"So God created humans to be like himself; he made men and women. God gave them his blessing and said, 'Have a lot of children! Fill the earth with people and bring it under your control' "* (Genesis 1:27–28a). The Lord had renewed these instructions to Noah and his family after the flood wiped out the rest of the human race (Genesis 9:1).

The post-flood generations, however, had adopted an all-for-one mentality, preferring to stay huddled together in Mesopotamia in the comfort of their commonality. God knew that eventually the people would be able to do anything they wanted. By removing the most important common ground of all—a shared language—God forced people to disperse.

BABYLON

Tower of Babel (1563)
Pieter Brueghel

13

Detail of a Babylonian city wall
in Pergamon Museum, Berlin

Ur

GENESIS 11:26–32

Most scholars agree that Ur was one of the oldest cities in southern Mesopotamia—built on the western banks of the Euphrates River. Later, the river changed course, and the city found itself ten miles from the waters of the Euphrates. Alternately, some scholars place the city in what is now northern Syria.

The geographical location of Ur matters less to the biblical story than its citizenry. Genesis 11–12 introduces the family of Terah, who lived in Ur. Terah had three sons: Nahor, Haran, and their older sibling—a man named Abram (later to be renamed Abraham).

For reasons known only to God, Abram was chosen to be the ancestor of a great nation—the patriarch of God's people—and to enjoy unimaginable blessing. Abram's story begins in Ur and continues through Scripture as his descendants alternate between obedience to God and unfaithfulness.

UR IN THE BIBLE

You are the LORD our God, the one who chose Abram— you brought him from Ur in Babylonia and named him Abraham. (Nehemiah 9:7)

■ *The city of Ur is mentioned four times in the Old Testament—all of them in reference to the fact that Abram and his family lived there when God first called them. Genesis 15:7 is typical of these references: "The LORD said to Abram, 'I brought you here from Ur in Chaldea, and I gave you this land' " (see also Genesis 11:26–28, 31; Nehemiah 9:7).*

Some scholars have suggested that the ziggurats of Mesopotamia—the most famous of which is found in Ur—influenced the construction of the tower of Babel. The builders' plans in Genesis 11:3— *"Let's build a city with a tower that reaches to the sky! We'll use hard bricks and tar instead of stone and mortar"*— are reminiscent of ziggurat construction techniques.

The ziggurat served as a temple, with a sanctuary on the ground floor and a sanctuary at the top, where the god to whom the temple was dedicated was thought to reside. The Ziggurat of Ur was dedicated to the moon god, the city's patron deity.

top: Ancient ziggurat at Ali Air Base, Iraq   bottom: *Temple and Palace Complex of Ur in Abraham's Time,* Balage Balogh

Haran

GENESIS 11:31–32; 24:1–67; 29:1—31:21

Haran, a city in northern Mesopotamia (approximately sixty miles north of where the Balikh and Euphrates Rivers meet), served as a staging area of sorts for Abram and his family. God called Abram to move from his homeland of Ur to a land God promised to Abram's descendants. Before reaching the promised land of Canaan, though, Abram and his family set up camp in Haran.

Traditional beehive house, Haran
© A.D. Riddle/BiblePlaces.com

The city of Haran shared a name with the surrounding region. Like other cities in this region (Peleg, Serug, Nahor, Terah), Haran was named for a member of Abram's family—in this case, his younger brother, the father of Lot.

Abram stayed in Haran until he was seventy-five years old. During that time, he amassed great wealth. When the time came to relocate to Canaan, Abram had a considerable household to move (Genesis 12:4–5).

The excavated remains of Haran belong to an Islamic town built on this site in the twelfth or thirteenth century AD. They provide a sense of the geography of Haran, but they do not date from the time of Abraham.

HARAN IN THE BIBLE

Terah decided to move from Ur to the land of Canaan. He took along Abram and Sarai and his grandson Lot, the son of Haran. But when they came to the city of Haran, they settled there instead. Terah lived to be 205 years old and died in Haran. (Genesis 11:31–32)

■ *The distance from Ur to Haran was approximately 550 miles.*

The region of Haran, which was also known as Paddan-Aram and Aram-Naharaim, figures prominently in several Bible stories. When the time came for Abraham's son Isaac to marry, Abraham sent his servant back to this region to find a suitable bride (Genesis 24:4,10).

Abraham's grandson Jacob fled to Haran to find refuge after deceiving his father Isaac and incurring the wrath of his brother Esau. While in Haran, Jacob married and fathered twelve sons—who would become the eponymous founders of the tribes of Israel. (Genesis 27:41—30:43; 35:16–26).

Haran excavations from the northwest
© A.D. Riddle/BiblePlaces.com

Introduction

The land of Canaan is as much of a character in the Old Testament as any human protagonist. It functions as a love interest of sorts for God's people—the object of desire that motivates them on their wearisome journey toward home.

We are first introduced to this "character" in the book of Genesis. God spoke to Abram—a man chosen for no discernible reason—telling him to leave everyone and everything he knew in Mesopotamia. God enlisted Abram to journey to a land prepared for him and his descendants—a place where God promised they would thrive for as long as they would remain faithful to him.

The book of Genesis traces Abram's nomadic journey through Canaan and details his encounters with the people—good and bad—who occupied the land. He got a taste of the land's beauty, as well as its harshness. For much of

Abraham and His Clan, Balage Balogh

Chapter 2

Canaan

the story, Abram remained an alien, a stranger in the land. Yet he recognized that one day his descendants would call this place home.

The seeds of Israel's eventual occupation of Canaan are sown in the stories of Isaac and Jacob, Abram's son and grandson, who roamed the land and settled in various places. Their triumphs and their struggle to embrace what it meant to be

God's chosen people set in motion the events that would shape their descendants for generations to come.

Genesis 12–50 follows Abram (later called Abraham), Isaac, and Jacob (and their families), beginning with their very first steps into the promised land. This chapter highlights nine important sites along the way.

Shechem

GENESIS 12:1–7

The patriarch Abram was seventy-five years old when God told him to leave his homeland in Haran. Abram's destination was Canaan, the land God had promised to him and his descendants. Abram packed up his family, his servants, and his possessions and headed southwest. The caravan traveled hundreds of miles until it reached the tree of Moreh, a shrine of sorts in the land of Shechem.

Shechem was located in a pass between Mount Ebal and Mount Gerizim. In that place, God appeared to Abram and renewed his promise to give Canaan to Abram's offspring. For the first time, Abram could see with his own eyes what God was offering—vast plains of fertile ground, a land of endless possibilities.

To commemorate his covenant with God, Abram built an altar at Shechem, thus establishing its significance to his descendants. Abram's grandson Jacob bought a plot of land in Shechem and built his own altar (Genesis 33:18–20). Later, the bones of Jacob's son Joseph were laid to rest there (Joshua 24:32).

After Joshua led the Israelites back into the promised land following a long period of captivity in Egypt, he assembled their tribal leaders at Shechem. There he renewed Israel's covenant with God (Joshua 24:1–27).

Today the site is known as Tell Balata and is located in the Palestinian West Bank, approximately forty miles north of Jerusalem. (*Tell* means "mount" or "mound" in Hebrew.)

SHECHEM IN THE BIBLE

When they came to the land of Canaan, Abram went as far as the sacred tree of Moreh in a place called Shechem. (Genesis 12:5b–6a)

Nablus (formerly known as Shechem), West Bank
View overlooking from Mount Gerizim

Shechem gained infamy as the site where Jacob's daughter Dinah was raped by the son of Hamor, the local ruler. After the attack, Hamor proposed that Jacob and his family intermarry with the people of the city. Jacob's sons replied that the men of Shechem had to be circumcised first. Eager to make allies of Jacob's family, the men agreed. While they were still recuperating from the painful procedure, two of Jacob's sons, Simeon and Levi, attacked and killed every male in Shechem to avenge their sister's rape (Genesis 34:1–31).

Generations later, when the tribes of Judah divided the promised land, Shechem was allotted to Manasseh, though it shared a border with Ephraim (Joshua 17:7–8).

left: Ruins of Shechem, Israel, the High Place.

Negev

GENESIS 12:9; 13:1–4

Shaped like an inverted triangle, the southernmost part of modern-day Israel is known as the Negev (*Negeb*) or Southern Desert. The word *Negeb* means "dry, parched, south country." True to its name, the region supports only the sparsest of vegetation: occasional acacia trees and wildflowers.

Despite the harsh climate, permanent settlements have existed in the Negev for thousands of years, primarily near trade routes that connected Egypt to its neighbors on the Asian continent. The Old Testament patriarch Abram used one of these routes to escape to Egypt when a famine struck the promised land (Genesis 12:10).

Some three hundred years after Abram trekked across the Southern Desert, Moses led Abram's descendants through the same region. Their journey lasted almost forty years—God's punishment for their lack of faith after he delivered them from slavery in Egypt. Before they could enter the promised land of Canaan, they were forced to wander in the barren wilderness of the Negev.

Though conditions were far less than ideal, God cared for the Israelites in the Negev. He caused manna (bread from heaven) to fall like dew on the ground almost every morning. He brought forth water from rocks for the people to drink (Exodus 16:1—17:7). In the foreboding landscape of the Southern Desert, God's people learned to trust him.

NEGEV IN THE BIBLE

Abram and Sarai took everything they owned and went to the Southern Desert. Lot went with them. Abram was very rich. He owned many cattle, sheep, and goats, and had a lot of silver and gold. Abram moved from place to place in the Southern Desert. (Genesis 13:1–3a)

Before the Israelites reclaimed the promised land, Moses sent in spies to get the lay of the land. According to the spies' report, the Amalekites—a seminomadic people and later an occasional enemy of the Israelites—lived in the Southern Desert (Numbers 13:29).

Later in Israel's history, kings built small villages and fortresses in the Negev to protect the kingdom's southern border.

background: Negev Desert
Geological park in Timna, Israel

Beersheba

GENESIS 21:22–34

Beersheba was the southernmost city in the official kingdom of Israel. To its south lay the desolate Southern (Negev) Desert.

First Samuel 8:1–3 reveals that Joel and Abijah, the sons of Samuel, served as judges in Beersheba. Unlike their father, who was revered by the people, Joel and Abijah were known for being corrupt—always willing to accept bribes and pervert justice.

Hundreds of years later, the prophet Amos called out Beersheba as a center of idol worship (Amos 5:5; 8:14).

Despite its proximity to the desert, Beersheba was habitable thanks to an underground water supply. While living in the region with his family, Abraham dug a well from which to draw water. Shortly thereafter, a dispute arose with Abimelech, the king of neighboring Gerar, as to who owned the well. Abraham offered the king seven lambs to settle the dispute, and the two made a treaty. The city's name was derived from their dispute. The Hebrew word *beer* means "well," and the word *sheba* means "seven."

Abraham spent his final years in Beersheba. His son Isaac put down roots there by digging a well of his own and building an altar to the Lord (Genesis 26:23–33).

Years later, Beersheba was the site of a grand deception by Jacob, Isaac's son. By posing as his older brother Esau, Jacob tricked Isaac into giving him Esau's birthright and blessing. Esau vowed revenge, so Jacob was forced to flee for his life (Genesis 27:1–45).

Jacob returned to Beersheba—briefly—as an old man, during his trip to Egypt, where he was to be reunited with his long-lost son Joseph. At Beersheba, Jacob worshiped God by offering sacrifices. God spoke to him and promised to go with him on his journey (Genesis 46:1–4).

BEERSHEBA IN THE BIBLE

Abraham planted a tamarisk tree in Beersheba and worshiped the eternal Lord God. Then Abraham lived a long time as a foreigner in the land of the Philistines. (Genesis 21:33–34)

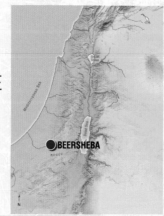

BEERSHEBA

© BiblePlaces.com

Variations of the phrase *"from Dan in the north to Beersheba in the south"* are used throughout the Old Testament in reference to the united nation of Israel (see 2 Samuel 3:9–10; 17:11; 24:2, 15; 1 Kings 4:25; 2 Chronicles 30:5). Dan, Beersheba's northern counterpart, was located about twenty-five miles north of the Sea of Galilee. The distance from Dan to Beersheba is approximately 144 miles.

Bethel

GENESIS 12:8; 13:3–18; 28:10–22

Most scholars think the Old Testament city of Bethel was located in central Israel, approximately twenty miles west-northwest of the Dead Sea's northern shore—the site of the modern Arab village of Beitin. Dissenting scholars believe the city was located in the Negev Desert region of Canaan.

Bethel played an important role in Jewish history. Of all the cities in the Old Testament, only Jerusalem is mentioned more often. Abram built an altar at Bethel (though it was known as Luz at the time) during his journey through Canaan. It was in this region that Abram and his nephew Lot parted ways because the land could not sustain their combined herds and flocks.

The patriarch most closely associated with Bethel is Jacob, Abram's grandson. While on the run from his brother, Jacob camped overnight near Luz. He used a rock for a pillow and dreamed of a ladder reaching to heaven, with angels ascending and descending. Standing beside the ladder was God himself. In the dream, God renewed his covenant with Jacob's family—Abraham's descendants—to give them the land of Canaan.

To show his gratitude and celebrate the fact that God had come to him, Jacob built a memorial using the rock he'd slept on. He renamed the city "Bethel," which is Hebrew for "house of God."

BETHEL IN THE BIBLE

When Jacob got up early the next morning, he took the rock that he had used for a pillow and stood it up as a place of worship. Then he poured olive oil on the rock to dedicate it to God, and he named the place Bethel. Before that it had been named Luz.
(Genesis 28:18–19)

According to Judges 20:26–28, the ark of the covenant (or sacred chest), the physical symbol of God's presence among the Israelites, was kept in Bethel for a time. The esteemed judge Samuel made many regular visits there.

Years later, the city's reputation changed for the worse. During the reign of Jeroboam I, Bethel was used as a sanctuary—a place where the king could indulge in idol worship (1 Kings 12:26–33).

Sodom and Gomorrah

GENESIS 13:10–13; 18:16–33; 19:1–29

Sodom and Gomorrah are the two best-known "cities of the valley" mentioned in Genesis 19:29. (The others were Zoar, Admah, and Zeboiim.) The definitive location of these cities has not been determined. However, they are generally associated with the Dead Sea, particularly the region south and east of the sea.

The Dead Sea is so named because it cannot support any aquatic life, aside from bacteria and parasites. The level of salt is so high that any fish in it would die almost immediately. The Dead Sea has no outlet. Water flows into it but does not flow out. That, combined with a rapid rate of evaporation, accounts for its high salt content.

That didn't stop people from building cities in its vicinity. Many scholars think the cities of Sodom and Gomorrah were built somewhere nearby. In time, these cities developed a reputation for extreme wickedness. Despite their notoriety, Abraham's nephew Lot chose to settle near Sodom after parting ways with his uncle (Genesis 13:12–13).

In Genesis 18:16–33, God revealed to Abraham his plan to destroy Sodom and Gomorrah for their inhabitants' sinfulness. Abraham pleaded with God to spare the cities if only ten righteous people could be found there. Alas, ten could not be found.

God sent two angels to Sodom to warn Lot and his family of the coming judgment. God gave Lot and his family a chance to escape to nearby Zoar, and then he rained judgment on Sodom and Gomorrah in the form of burning sulfur. Both cities were utterly destroyed.

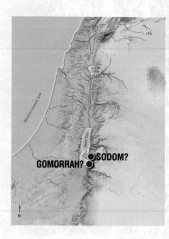

GOMORRAH? SODOM?

SODOM AND GOMORRAH
IN THE BIBLE

The sun was coming up as Lot reached the town of Zoar, and the LORD sent burning sulfur down like rain on Sodom and Gomorrah. He destroyed those cities and everyone who lived in them, as well as their land and the trees and grass that grew there. (Genesis 19:23–25)

God's messenger issued three instructions to Lot's family as the destruction of Sodom and Gomorrah began: *"Run for your lives! Don't even look back. And don't stop in the valley. Run to the hills, where you will be safe"* (Genesis 19:17). When the family reached Zoar, Lot's wife turned to look at the destruction of Sodom and Gomorrah and immediately was reduced to a pillar of salt. Even today, salt formations in the region can be found, serving as reminders of her fateful choice.

Sodom and Gomorrah's infamy long outlived their actual existence. Their fate served as a caution to all wicked people. In Deuteronomy 29:22–23, Moses warned the Israelites of the consequences of breaking their covenant with God: *"The Lord will strike your country with diseases and disasters. . . . It will be as lifeless as the land around the cities of Sodom, Gomorrah, Admah, and Zeboiim, after the Lord became angry and destroyed them."*

Jesus himself referred to the doomed cities when he sent out his disciples. Regarding any town that would not welcome his followers, Jesus said, *"I promise you the day of judgment will be easier for the towns of Sodom and Gomorrah than for that town"* (Matthew 10:15).

Mamre at Hebron

GENESIS 13:18; 23:1–20; 25:7–11

After Abram parted company with his nephew Lot, the patriarch moved to the southern hill country of Canaan, approximately twenty miles south-southwest of modern-day Jerusalem.

Mamre is where God told Abram (recently renamed Abraham) that his wife Sarah would give birth to their long-awaited son (Genesis 18:1–15). It is also where Abraham begged God not to destroy Sodom and Gomorrah (Genesis 18:16–33).

When Abram achieved a military victory and rescued his nephew Lot, who had been captured by a coalition led by the king of Elam, Abram built an altar and set up camp in Mamre, a place named for one of Abram's allies in the battle (Genesis 14:1–24).

Mamre is usually associated with the neighboring city of Hebron, one of the oldest continually inhabited cities in the promised land (Numbers 13:22). The city was originally known as Kiriath-Arba (Genesis 23:2).

Mamre is the location of Machpelah Cave, where Abraham and Sarah, Abraham's son Isaac and his wife Rebekah, and Isaac's son Jacob and his wife Leah are all buried (see pages 38–39 for more on Machpelah Cave).

Hundreds of years after Abraham died, the Israelites, led by Moses, returned to Canaan. Before they entered the land, Moses sent spies to scope it out. The first place the spies came to was Hebron. By that time, Hebron had become a heavily fortified city, inhabited by large, physically imposing people. When the spies saw the city and its inhabitants, most of them lost their nerve for entering the promised land (Numbers 13:1–33).

Eventually, Joshua led the Israelites to victory against the people of Hebron—and against other cities in the region (Joshua 10:1–15). He gave Hebron to Caleb, one of the spies who did not lose his nerve (Joshua 14:6–15).

Hundreds of years later, David found allies in Hebron while on the run from King Saul. To reward the kindness he found in Hebron, David sent the city a portion of the plunder he and his men collected from their battles with their enemies the Amalekites (1 Samuel 30:26–31). In time, David was crowned king of Judah in Hebron and lived there for seven and a half years (2 Samuel 2:1–11).

MAMRE AT HEBRON
IN THE BIBLE

Abram took down his tents and went to live near the sacred trees of Mamre at Hebron, where he built an altar in honor of the LORD.
(Genesis 13:18)

MAMRE

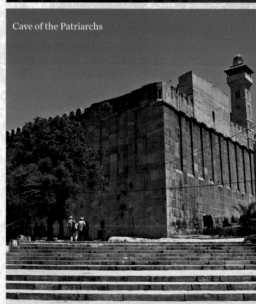

Cave of the Patriarchs

Hebron city divided between Jews and Arabs

Gerar

GENESIS 20:1–18; 26:1–31

The location of Gerar remains a mystery. Nothing in the biblical narrative indicates a definitive placement of the town. Four possible sites have been proposed by scholars. Of them, Tel Haror in southern Canaan—approximately fifty miles southwest of modern-day Jerusalem—is the most widely accepted.

Gerar was the site of two of the strangest deceptions recorded in Scripture. When Abraham and his beautiful wife Sarah stopped there on their journey through the promised land, Abraham was afraid Abimelech, the king of Gerar, would kill him in order to take Sarah as his own wife. So Abraham told the king that Sarah was his sister. Thinking Sarah was unmarried, Abimelech sent for her.

A short time later, God spoke to Abimelech in two dreams, warning him that he and his people would be killed unless he returned Sarah, a married woman, to her husband. Shaken, the king sent for Abraham, who owned up to his deception. In order to appease God, the king showered Abraham with gifts and gave him his choice of land in Gerar.

Years later, Abraham's son Isaac went to Gerar to find relief from a famine. When the men of the town started asking about his wife Rebekah, Isaac told them she was his sister. The king of Gerar, Abimelech (who was likely the son or grandson of the same-named king that Abraham dealt with), spotted Isaac caressing Rebekah and realized she was his wife. The king sent word that no one was to lay a hand on Isaac or Rebekah.

Like father, like son.

GERAR IN THE BIBLE

Once during Abraham's lifetime, the fields had not produced enough grain, and now the same thing happened. So Isaac went to King Abimelech of the Philistines in the land of Gerar, because the LORD had appeared to Isaac and said: "Isaac, stay away from Egypt! I will show you where I want you to go. You will live there as a foreigner, but I will be with you and bless you. I will keep my promise to your father Abraham by giving this land to you and your descendants." (Genesis 26:1–3)

Isaac settled in Gerar and thrived—so much so that his neighbors began to resent him. They filled in all his wells with dirt. Anxious, the king of Gerar asked Isaac to leave Gerar. Isaac complied and settled in a nearby valley. But that did not stop the disputes. Every time Isaac dug a well, the herdsmen of Gerar would claim it as their own.

Abimelech was smart enough to recognize that God was with Isaac. Eager to put the conflicts behind them, Abimelech proposed a treaty. Isaac agreed and continued to thrive in the region outside of Gerar.

Gilead

GENESIS 31:22–55; SONG OF SONGS 6:5;
JEREMIAH 8:22; 46:11

Gilead was a mountainous region in the Transjordan (the area east of the Jordan River), southeast of the Sea of Galilee, bordered by Bashan on the north and Mishor on the south. The Jabbok River flowed through the middle of Gilead, effectively dividing the region in half.

Gilead was fertile, covered with forests. The King's Highway, one of the major roads in Old Testament times, ran through the region. The fact that the people of Gilead controlled the route gave them power in the ancient world. Today the kingdom of Jordan occupies the area where the forests of Gilead once stood.

Gilead figures prominently in the story of Laban's pursuit of Jacob (the son of Isaac and grandson of Abraham). Laban was Jacob's father-in-law, though their relationship was less than familial. Jacob had worked for Laban for twenty years and had married two of Laban's daughters. Yet Jacob felt that Laban had been cheating him, so he packed up his family and left—without telling Laban. Laban gave chase and overtook Jacob's caravan in the hill country of Gilead. There the two men made peace and built a pillar to commemorate the event.

Hundreds of years later, Moses led the Israelites in wresting control of the southern half of Gilead from Sihon, the king of Heshbon (Deuteronomy 2:26–37). He then led them in a campaign against Og, the king of Bashan, for control of the northern half of Gilead (Deuteronomy 3:1–10).

GILEAD IN THE BIBLE

Turn away your eyes—they make me melt. Your hair tosses about as gracefully as goats coming down from Gilead. (Song of Songs 6:5)

Gilead is perhaps best known in Scripture for its medicinal products and services (Jeremiah 8:22). The people in the region made and exported a certain balm, a resin produced from local pine and cedar trees that was used to soothe wounds—specifically those involving a loss of skin.

The balm was so popular that it was referred to in ancient proverbs. God instructed the prophet Jeremiah to issue this warning: *"Egypt, no medicine can heal you, not even the soothing lotion from Gilead"* (Jeremiah 46:11).

Sacred Burial Places

GENESIS 23:1–20; 35:16–29

Abraham's wife Sarah died at the age of 127 in Kiriath-Arba, also known as Hebron (see page 32 for more information on Hebron). Abraham, a stranger to the land, had to negotiate with the resident Hittites for a place to bury her.

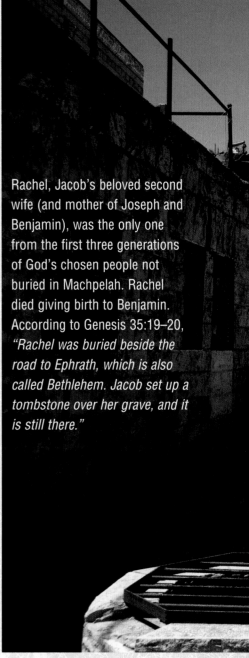

He chose a site known as Machpelah Cave, which sat at the end of a field, and he purchased it from its owner for 400 pieces of silver.

There Abraham buried his beloved wife Sarah. When Abraham died at the age of 175, his sons Isaac and Ishmael buried him in Machpelah. When Isaac died at the age of 180, his sons Esau and Jacob buried him in Machpelah. Isaac's wife Rebekah was also buried there. When Jacob died in Egypt, his twelve sons accompanied his body to Hebron to bury him in Machpelah. Finally, Jacob's first wife, Leah, was buried there (Genesis 49:31).

Rachel, Jacob's beloved second wife (and mother of Joseph and Benjamin), was the only one from the first three generations of God's chosen people not buried in Machpelah. Rachel died giving birth to Benjamin. According to Genesis 35:19–20, *"Rachel was buried beside the road to Ephrath, which is also called Bethlehem. Jacob set up a tombstone over her grave, and it is still there."*

MACHPELAH IN THE BIBLE

So Abraham buried his wife Sarah in Machpelah Cave that was in the field he had bought from the Hittites.
(Genesis 23:19–20)

© BiblePlaces.com

HEBRON

Herod, who reigned as king of the Jews for the Roman Empire from 37 BC to 4 BC, oversaw the construction of large, beautiful stone walls around Machpelah Cave. The cenotaphs (empty tombs) of the patriarchs and matriarchs of Israel are housed in separate octagonal chambers in three major rooms. The cenotaphs of Abraham and Sarah are located in the middle of the site. The cenotaphs of Isaac and Rebekah are located on the east side, and those of Jacob and Leah are located on the west side.

The site, located in modern-day Hebron, is revered not only by Jews and Christians but by Muslims as well, who refer to it as the Sanctuary of Abraham or Ibrahimi Mosque. Control of the site has been hotly contested for decades. Today, because the cenotaphs of Isaac and Rebekah lie in an area fully controlled by the Palestinians, Jewish people may visit there only ten days a year.

Introduction

The journey of Abraham's descendants to the land God had promised was anything but a direct route. One major detour had its origins in a tragic sibling rivalry among the twelve sons of Abraham's grandson Jacob.

Jacob and his family were living in Canaan at the time. Jacob's blatant favoritism toward Joseph, his eleventh son—but firstborn by his beloved wife Rachel—was the cause of bad blood between Joseph and his brothers. Jacob showered Joseph with gifts and affection, much to his brothers' displeasure. The fact that Joseph told his brothers of his dreams, which involved them bowing down to him, inflamed them even more.

One day Joseph was sent by his father to check up on his brothers who were taking care of their

sheep. When they saw Joseph coming, they made plans to kill him. However, instead of killing him, they decided to sell him as a slave to a caravan of traveling merchants. The caravan made its way to Egypt, the powerful kingdom that bordered Canaan on the southwest.

Joseph's life in Egypt is one of Scripture's great rags-to-riches stories. After being sold as a slave to a royal official named Potiphar, Joseph was falsely accused of attempted rape by Potiphar's wife and thrown into prison.

While he was incarcerated, Joseph made the acquaintance of the king's personal servant (or cupbearer) and chief cook. They had been imprisoned for displeasing Pharaoh, the king of Egypt. Both the cupbearer and cook had dreams

Egypt

loaded with symbolism, Joseph, who had a gift from God for understanding the meaning of dreams, was able to interpret their dreams.

Joseph told the cupbearer he would be released and restored to his old job. The cook's dream meant that he would be executed. And that's exactly what happened.

Two years later, Pharaoh himself began having troubling dreams. The cupbearer remembered Joseph and recommended him to Pharaoh. Joseph successfully interpreted the king's dreams, which warned that Egypt would experience seven years of abundance followed by seven years of famine. Joseph instructed Pharaoh to put someone in charge of famine preparation. Pharaoh chose Joseph. In one day, Joseph went

from being an imprisoned slave to the second-in-command over all Egypt.

Joseph supervised the collection and storage of food during Egypt's years of plenty. When famine struck as predicted, the Egyptian people survived on the surplus. In fact, people from across the region came to Egypt for food. Among them were Joseph's brothers, who were stunned to see Joseph in a position of power. They had no choice but to bow to him, just as Joseph's dream had predicted.

Instead of exacting revenge, Joseph arranged for his entire family to move to Egypt in order to escape the famine. That's how the people of Israel came to be in Egypt.

Goshen

GENESIS 47:1–12; EXODUS 1:1–22

After Joseph reunited with his family, he wanted to make sure they were cared for through the remaining years of famine. The best way to do that was to relocate them to Egypt, where he could personally oversee their care. Pharaoh permitted Joseph's family to settle in Goshen, one of Egypt's most fertile areas.

Also known as the District of Rameses, Goshen lay in the eastern Nile delta, northwest of the modern-day Gulf of Suez. The region was set apart from the rest of Egypt because of its distance from the Nile irrigation canals that connected the kingdom.

The land was perfect for grazing. When Joseph's brothers identified themselves to Pharaoh as shepherds, he knew exactly where to send them. In fact, the separation of Goshen from the rest of Egypt suited both the Egyptians and Joseph's family. Egyptians didn't like to associate with shepherds, and Joseph's family was able to thrive without the rulers of Egypt paying them much attention.

Exodus 1 picks up the story some 300 years later—when things had changed drastically. The descendants of Joseph's family—the Hebrew people—still lived in Goshen, but now as slaves of Egypt. The Egyptians, afraid of being overrun by the proliferating Hebrews, enslaved them and put them to work building cities. At one point, the Egyptian king ordered that all male Hebrew newborns be drowned in the Nile River.

Life in Goshen was miserable for the Hebrews, who prayed fervently for God to deliver them.

Joseph took five of his brothers to the king and told him, "My father and my brothers have come from Canaan. They have brought their sheep, goats, cattle, and everything else they own to the region of Goshen."
(Genesis 47:1–2)

The Hebrew people lived in Egypt for approximately 430 years (Exodus 12:40).

Fields of Nile Delta near Tanis
© BiblePlaces.com

GOSHEN IN THE BIBLE

The king said to Joseph, "It's good that your father and brothers have arrived. I will let them live anywhere they choose in the land of Egypt, but I suggest that they settle in Goshen, the best part of our land. I would also like for your finest shepherds to watch after my own sheep and goats." (Genesis 47:5–6)

Fields of Nile Delta with shelter near Tanis
© BiblePlaces.com

Fields near Tell el-Daba
© BiblePlaces.com

The Sinai Coast

EXODUS 13:17—14:31

God heard the cries of his people, who suffered terribly as slaves in Egypt. In response, he sent Moses to confront Pharaoh, king of Egypt, and demand that the Israelites be set free. When Pharaoh refused, God unleashed a series of plagues—ten in all—on Egypt. The first nine plagues didn't change Pharaoh's mind, but the tenth one—the death of every firstborn Egyptian son along with the firstborn male of every animal that belonged to the Egyptians—did.

The Crossing of the Red Sea, c. 1634. Nicholas Poussin (1594–1665).

The Israelites, who numbered over 600,000 men plus women and children, set out from Rameses, a city in Goshen. From there, God led them on a desert road down the western coast of the Sinai Peninsula, toward the Red Sea. The peninsula is bordered on the north by the Mediterranean Sea, on the south by the Red Sea, on the west by the Gulf of Suez, and on the east by the Gulf of Aqaba.

Tracing the exact route the Israelites followed out of Egypt is difficult. Theories abound as to the location of sites such as Succoth and Etham (Exodus 13:20), and Pi-Hahiroth, Baal-Zephon, and Migdol (Exodus 14:2).

What we do know is that shortly after the Israelites' departure, Pharaoh had yet another change of heart. Unwilling to lose his slave labor force, he gathered his chariot army and gave chase. The Israelites spotted their pursuers while they were camped next to a body of water that is traditionally associated with the Red Sea.

Panic ensued—until God sent a strong east wind to divide the waters and create a dry path for the Israelites to walk across. After the Israelites made it to the opposite shore, God closed the waters on the pursuing Egyptians, drowning them all.

The Israelites escaped from Egypt, and their journey to the promised land was about to begin.

SINAI
PENINSULA

Red Sea

SINAI COAST
IN THE BIBLE

But the king's horses and chariots and soldiers caught up with them while they were camping by the Red Sea near Pi-Hahiroth and Baal-Zephon. (Exodus 14:9)

The most direct route from Egypt to Canaan was through the land of the Philistines (Exodus 13:17), which ran along the southern coast of the Mediterranean Sea. However, that path would have taken them through Philistine territory, so God took them on a safer, albeit more circuitous, route.

The Sinai Desert and Mountains

EXODUS 15:22—20:26; 32:1–35

Free from the Egyptians, the Israelites took the long way through the Sinai Peninsula on their way to the promised land of Canaan. One of their first stops was Marah, a place known for its pools of bitter water. When the Israelites complained about having nothing to drink, God told Moses to throw a piece of wood into the water, which made it sweet. The exact location of Marah remains a mystery, though it may have been modern-day Ain Hawarah, about fifty miles south-southwest of the northern end of the Gulf of Suez.

After leaving Marah, the Israelites camped at the oasis of Elim, which had twelve springs and seventy palm trees. Many scholars identify Elim with the region seven miles south of Ain Hawarah. From Elim, the Israelites made their way across the western edge of the Sinai Desert. When the people grumbled about being hungry, God sent manna (bread from heaven) and quail to feed them.

Their next stop was Rephidim, a location that has not been definitively identified—though some scholars associate it with modern-day Wadi Refayid. When no water was found there, God told Moses to strike a rock with his walking stick. Water poured from the rock.

The Israelites moved next to the Desert of Sinai, in the southeast region of the peninsula, and set up camp at the foot of Mount Sinai— also known as Mount Horeb in Hebrew (Exodus 3:1; 33:6). Scholars disagree as to the actual location of Mount Sinai, though many identify it with Jebel Musa (Arabic for "Mountain of Moses") in southern central Sinai. Today the Monastery of Saint Catherine sits at the foot of this mountain.

God called Moses to the top of Mount Sinai and initiated the covenant relationship with the Israelites. The Ten Commandments, which the Israelites would be required to follow, were written by God onto two stone tablets. God's laws and instructions comprise almost the entire second half of the book of Exodus.

Rephidim was the site of the Israelites' first battle on their way to the promised land. While the Amalekites attacked the Israelites, Moses stood on a hill overlooking the battle. When he raised his hands, the Israelites gained the upper hand in battle. When he lowered them, the Amalekites took control. With the help of two assistants, Moses managed to keep his hands up until the Israelites were victorious (Exodus 17:8–16).

SINAI IN THE BIBLE

On the fifteenth day of the second month after the Israelites had escaped from Egypt, they left Elim and started through the western edge of the Sinai Desert in the direction of Mount Sinai. (Exodus 16:1)

Mount Sinai was the site of the Israelites' first recorded dalliance with idol worship after leaving Egypt. When Moses didn't return from the mountain right away, the Israelites assumed the worst and demanded that Aaron, Moses' brother, make an idol they could worship. Aaron melted down gold jewelry and cast it in the shape of a young bull. That's what the people were worshiping when Moses finally returned (Exodus 32:1–35).

SINAI
DESERT &
MOUNTAINS

MOUNT SINAI?

Red Sea

St. Catherine's Monastery

House inside St. Catherine's Monastery

A narrow sandstone canyon in the Sinai Desert

Introduction

The first forays of God's people into Canaan were both exploratory and transitory. Abraham, Isaac, and Jacob had wandered the breadth and width of the land as nomads. They had interacted with its inhabitants as visitors, not as owners. They had set up semi-permanent camps—for years at a time in some places—but they were always attuned to God's call, always ready to move on to the next destination.

In contrast, the return to Canaan led by Moses, and later by Joshua, was a sustained campaign. The Israelites came to claim what was rightfully theirs—and to conquer anyone who stood in their way.

That's what was supposed to happen, at least. God wanted his people to march boldly into their land, remove the other nations that had settled there, and enjoy the blessings that awaited them. Had the Israelites followed God's instructions, their story might have been much different.

The conquest of Canaan started promisingly enough, with decisive victories over Jericho, Ai, and the Amorites. Yet even within these stories of

Chapter 4

Conquest of Canaan

victory, telltale incidents of disobedience can be found:

■ A man named Achan tried to keep for himself the spoils of victory that belonged to God.

■ After defeating the Amorites, the Israelites allowed some of them to remain in the land instead of ridding themselves of their enemies once and for all.

Eventually, both incidents came back to haunt the Israelites.

The conquest of Canaan under Joshua petered out shortly after the Israelites had claimed the central hill country and the Southern (Negev) Desert region for themselves. The Israelites' failure to clear the land completely set the stage for later conflicts under Kings David and Solomon.

Jericho in Joshua's Time, Balage Balogh

Jericho

JOSHUA 2–6

Many scholars believe Jericho is the oldest continuously occupied city in the world. Archaeologists have unearthed evidence of settlements dating back 11,000 years. The city is located in the Jordan Valley, about six miles north of the Dead Sea. Today it is identified with Tell es-Sultan.

In Joshua 1:4, God established the boundaries of the land he was giving the Israelites: *"It will reach from the Southern Desert to the Lebanon Mountains in the north, and to the northeast as far as the great Euphrates River. It will include the land of the Hittites, and the land from here at the Jordan River to the Mediterranean Sea on the west."* God promised Joshua that anywhere he stepped foot within those borders would belong to the Israelites. Joshua settled for the central hill country of Canaan and the Southern (Negev) Desert. The only two leaders of Israel who were able to conquer and hold the full extent of God's promised land were King David and his son Solomon.

Deuteronomy 34:3 refers to Jericho as "The City of Palm Trees" due to its tropical climate and vegetation. The city's most prominent feature was its fortification; walls surrounded the city to protect it from invasion. Despite their notoriety, these walls failed to prevent Jericho from becoming the first Canaanite city to fall to the Israelites.

God gave the people of Israel a taste of what lay in store for them as they approached the land of Canaan from the east. He blocked the waters of the Jordan River so they could cross on dry ground, similar to what he had done when they left Egypt. When the Israelites arrived at Jericho, God gave them detailed battle instructions. For six days in a row, the Israelites were to march once around the city in complete silence.

On the seventh day, they marched around the city seven times. After the seventh lap, the priests of Israel blasted their trumpets and the people gave a loud shout. That was all it took to bring down the walls of Jericho. The Israelites rushed in and utterly destroyed the city and its inhabitants.

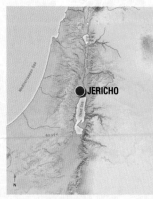

JERICHO

JERICHO IN THE BIBLE

The LORD said to Joshua: "With my help, you and your army will defeat the king of Jericho and his army, and you will capture the town. Here is how to do it: March slowly around Jericho once a day for six days. Take along the sacred chest and have seven priests walk in front of it, carrying trumpets." (Joshua 6:2–4a)

Jericho ranks second only to Jerusalem in the number of archaeological excavations because it contains some of the world's most important historic sites that are related to the Bible.

Modern-day Jericho

Excavations near Jericho of an ancient palace

Tower of Jericho,
Tell es-Sultan archaeological site, c. 7000 BC

Zacchaeus's sycamore tree in Jericho

According to the New Testament, Jesus was baptized in the Jordan River (Matthew 3:13–17) near Jericho. Many scholars believe Satan's temptation of Jesus (Matthew 4:1–11) took place on a mountain west of Jericho.

Jericho is also where the following episodes from Jesus' life took place:

- The healing of a blind man named Bartimaeus (Mark 10:46–52)

- Jesus' encounter with a tax collector named Zacchaeus (Luke 19:1–10)

Jericho is also mentioned as the setting for Jesus' parable of The Good Samaritan (Luke 10:25–37).

Jericho mudbrick wall
© BiblePlaces.com

Panorama of Jericho
© BiblePlaces.com

Ai

JOSHUA 7–8

The Israelites were feeling bold after conquering Jericho. Their next target was Ai, a town about fifteen miles away, just east of Bethel. Joshua sent an advance party of scouts to spy on the town, and they returned brimming with confidence. Their recommendation was to send a small army of 2,000–3,000 troops to take care of Ai while everyone else rested.

What they didn't know at the time was that a man in their midst, Achan, had taken some of the bounty of Jericho that belonged exclusively to God. As a result, the Lord's anger burned against the Israelites.

The small fighting force that attacked Ai was soundly defeated. Thirty-six Israelites were killed. The people's confidence evaporated. Joshua turned to God to find out what had gone wrong.

In accordance with God's instructions, Joshua ordered the Israelites to purify and present themselves to God. Achan admitted what he had done and was stoned to death.

With things set right, the Israelites prepared for a second attack on Ai. Joshua ordered 30,000 of his soldiers to stake out a position behind the city, under cover of darkness. He then led a force of 5,000 additional soldiers in a frontal assault on Ai. When the king of Ai saw them coming, he led his troops out to meet them in battle.

Joshua and his small force turned and ran at the sight of them, just like the Israelites had done in the first battle. The army of Ai gave chase, which allowed the 30,000 Israelites hiding behind the city to enter it unopposed and burn it to the ground.

Joshua and his smaller force then turned around and attacked their pursuers from one side while the forces that had laid waste to the city attacked from the other side. Over 12,000 inhabitants of Ai were killed, and the city was decimated.

Scholars have yet to reach a consensus on the location of Ai. Some identify it with the modern-day site of et-Tell. Yet historical and archaeological evidence suggests this particular site was uninhabited at the time the Israelites conquered Canaan. Other scholars believe the events of Joshua 8 took place in the neighboring city of Bethel.

AI IN THE BIBLE

While Israel was still camped near Jericho, Joshua sent some spies with these instructions: "Go to the town of Ai and find out whatever you can about the region around the town." The spies left and went to Ai, which is east of Bethel and near Beth-Aven. They went back to Joshua and reported, "You don't need to send the whole army to attack Ai—2,000 or 3,000 troops will be enough. Why bother the whole army for a town that small?" (Joshua 7:2–3)

Upper and lower photos: Vicinity surrounding Ai

The descendants of Ai are mentioned in the list of exiles who returned to Jerusalem with Zerubbabel and Nehemiah (Ezra 2:28; Nehemiah 7:32).

Gibeon

JOSHUA 9

Word spread throughout Canaan of the invading force that had destroyed Jericho and Ai, so a number of Canaanite nations decided to join together to repel the invasion and defeat the Israelites. The people of Gibeon, however, chose a different tactic.

The treaty with the Gibeonites stood for centuries until it was broken by King Saul. The Bible does not describe the exact circumstances. Second Samuel 21:1a simply says, *"Saul and his family are guilty of murder, because he had the Gibeonites killed."*

As a result of breaking the treaty, Israel experienced three years of famine during David's reign. To even the score, the Gibeonites demanded that seven of Saul's heirs be handed over to them. David complied, and Saul's heirs were put to death (2 Samuel 21:2–9).

Gibeon was a town in central Canaan—and likely the dominant partner in a confederation of neighboring towns. Today Gibeon is identified with el-Jib, located just north of Jerusalem.

The Gibeonites abandoned their confederacy to enter into a treaty with the Israelites. In order to do so, the Gibeonites needed to convince the Israelites that they were from a far-off land. (The Israelites would not have been receptive to a treaty with a local nation.)

To sell their ruse, the Gibeonites loaded their donkeys with worn-out bags, old wineskins, and dry, crumbly bread. They put on worn clothes and old sandals. They gave themselves the appearance of travelers who had come a great distance.

The Israelites were suspicious, but eventually they agreed to a peace treaty—without consulting God first. The treaty offered protection for the Gibeonites in exchange for their servitude.

A few days later, the Israelites discovered that the people with whom they had made this treaty actually lived nearby, in Gibeon and the surrounding towns. The Israelites were unhappy with the Gibeonites, but they honored their treaty and did not attack. Instead they cursed the Gibeonites with two of the most labor-intensive tasks in the Israelite culture: cutting firewood for offerings on the Lord's altar and carrying water for the priests.

GIBEON IN THE BIBLE

The people of Gibeon had also heard what Joshua had done to Jericho and Ai. (Joshua 9:3)

Shortly after David's son Solomon was crowned king, he traveled to Gibeon to offer a sacrifice. While there, God vowed to grant Solomon anything he requested. Solomon asked for the wisdom to lead the nation of Israel—a request that pleased God greatly (1 Kings 3:4–15).

The Aijalon Valley

JOSHUA 10:1–15

The alliance between the Israelites and the Gibeonites was cause for great concern among the other nations of Canaan. The kings of Jerusalem, Hebron, Jarmuth, Lachish, and Eglon—collectively known as the five Amorite kings—joined forces to attack Gibeon for conspiring with the Israelites.

THE AIJALON VALLEY
IN THE BIBLE

The LORD was helping the Israelites defeat the Amorites that day. So about noon, Joshua prayed to the LORD loud enough for the Israelites to hear: "Our LORD, make the sun stop in the sky over Gibeon, and the moon stand still over Aijalon Valley." So the sun and the moon stopped and stood still until Israel defeated its enemies. This poem can be found in The Book of Jashar. *The sun stood still and didn't go down for about a whole day.* (Joshua 10:12–13)

The Gibeonites sent a call for help to their new ally, and the Israelites responded immediately. Joshua marched his entire army approximately twenty miles west-southwest from Gilgal to Gibeon—a steep, uphill climb. The Israelites arrived early in the morning, perhaps while the moon was still out, and caught the Amorite forces by surprise. The rout was on.

The surviving Amorite forces fled to Beth-Horon, a city about five miles northwest of Gibeon, and then down into the Aijalon Valley. (The site is identified today as Yalo, a Palestinian village located about eight miles from Ramla in the West Bank.)

The Lord slowed the Amorites' progress considerably by allowing large hailstones to pummel them. (According to Joshua 10:11, more Amorite soldiers were killed by the hailstones than by the Israelites' swords.)

THE AIJALON VALLEY

Joshua offered a strategic prayer to ensure that his men could finish the battle. He asked God to make the sun stand still over Gibeon and the moon stand still over the Aijalon Valley. God honored Joshua's request and allowed the Israelites to chase down and kill the Amorite kings and decimate their armies. In the process, he immeasurably bolstered the Israelites' intimidation factor among the other nations of Canaan.

According to 1 Samuel 14:31, the Aijalon Valley was the site of another memorable Israelite victory. After Jonathan, the son of King Saul, launched a daring attack on a Philistine encampment, the Philistines lost their nerve and fled. King Saul and his army, recognizing the opportunity to score a decisive victory over their enemies, gave chase. They caught up with the Philistines and defeated them in the Aijalon Valley.

Introduction

At first glance, the decision to establish a monarchy just like all the other nations seems to have been just what Israel needed. The Israelites rallied behind King Saul and King David as they battled the Canaanite nations for control of the promised land. Their military excursions were successful, for the most part. Piece by piece, the Israelites removed the obstacles that stood in their way and claimed the land God had given them. At the zenith of the monarchy, under King Solomon, the Israelites staked boundaries at the farthest reaches of Canaan.

Take a closer look at the Old Testament narrative, though, and you'll see that Israel's shift toward monarchy was actually the beginning of the end for the nation. Israel's original theocratic government—the fact that God himself dictated national policy—is what set it apart from other nations. No other nation could claim the kind of divine direction that ancient Israel enjoyed. The people of Israel weren't called "God's people" for nothing!

The Kingdom of Israel

Tower of David, Jerusalem

Yet divine direction wasn't what they wanted. Uniqueness was not their goal. The Israelites looked at the other nations around them—ones led by fallible human kings—and decided they were missing out by not having royalty of their own. So, awkward though it may have been, they took their request for a human king to their divine King. And in a textbook example of the truism "Be careful what you wish for," God gave Israel a succession of kings. Some were good; some were ineffective; some were evil. In general, things were a far cry from what might have been

If the Bible teaches us anything, it's that rejecting God always brings negative consequences. To chart the downhill trajectory of Israel during its monarchy, we need only to look at the people's relationship with the land. When the Israelites obeyed God, they enjoyed peace and prosperity. They reaped the natural goodness of a land that flowed with milk and honey. When they disobeyed God—when they tolerated idolatry and injustice instead of opposing them—God allowed Israel's enemies to invade and conquer. God allowed his people to lose control of the

SACRED SITES IN THE BIBLE

After Israel had captured the land, they met at Shiloh and set up the sacred tent. (Joshua 18:1)

MOUNT EBAL
MOUNT GERIZIM

According to Jeremiah 7:12, Shiloh was destroyed because of the wickedness of its people. It was rebuilt after the Israelites returned from exile in Babylon.

Mount Ebal
© BiblePlaces.com

Early Sacred Sites

EXODUS 40:1–38; DEUTERONOMY 11:1–32;
JOSHUA 8:30–35; 18:1; 1 SAMUEL 1:1–28

Before the temple was built, God dwelled among his people in the tabernacle, or sacred tent,—a temporary, portable home for God's presence. The tabernacle had accompanied the Israelites through the wilderness.

Later, God chose specific locations in and around Canaan from which to guide, bless, and correct his people. Many of those places subsequently took on great significance for the Israelites.

For example, God chose the neighboring peaks of Mount Gerizim and Mount Ebal as the locations from which his blessings and curses would be pronounced as the Israelites entered the promised land. The peaks of Mount Ebal and Mount Gerizim form either side of the pass through Shechem into Canaan—Ebal on the north, Gerizim on the south. They are located near the modern-day West Bank city of Nablus.

God wanted the Israelites to know what was at stake as they crossed the border into their new land. If they obeyed him, they would be blessed beyond any nation on earth. If they disobeyed, they would face his judgment.

After the Israelites conquered the Canaanite cities of Jericho and Ai, Joshua led the people back to these twin mountains. There he built an altar to the Lord, and the blessings and curses of the Law were read once again.

Shiloh, a town located in the hills of Ephraim about ten miles north of Bethel, became a sacred site to the Israelites shortly after they entered the promised land. Shiloh was chosen as the site where the tabernacle would be housed, along with the sacred chest (ark of the covenant). The town also became a headquarters for the priests of Israel. Shiloh served as the capital of Israel until the temple was built in Jerusalem during Solomon's reign. Today the ancient site of Shiloh is identified with Khirbet Seilun.

Mount Gerizim
© BiblePlaces.com

THE LAND OF THE PHILISTINES
IN THE BIBLE

The Philistines took the sacred chest from near Ebenezer to the town of Ashdod. (1 Samuel 5:1)

© BiblePlaces.com

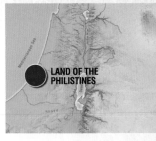

LAND OF THE PHILISTINES

According to Judges 3:1–4, God allowed the Philistines to stay in Canaan in order to teach successive generations of Israelites proper fighting techniques for use in war. The Philistines were excellent instructors. The Israelites and Philistines waged war against each other from the time of the judges Shamgar and Samson all the way to the reign of King Hezekiah during the divided monarchy (2 Kings 18:8).

The Land of the Philistines

1 SAMUEL 4–7

The Philistines migrated to Canaan around 1200 BC, most likely coming from the Greek mainland and Aegean Islands. Prone to war, the Philistines launched an offensive on Egypt—and lost. Ramses, the pharaoh of Egypt, settled the Philistines on the southeastern coast of the Mediterranean Sea

■ *The first reference to the Philistines in Scripture is found in Genesis 10:14, where they are listed among the descendants of Ham, Noah's son.*

Ashdod-Yam fortress (Kalat al-Mina), Ashdod, Israel. Photo by Bukvoed.

The Philistines consolidated the region, which extended roughly from modern-day Tel Aviv to Gaza. Five major Philistine cities ("the Pentapolis") were established: Ekron, Ashdod, Gaza, Ashkelon, and Gath. Ekron is identified with modern-day Tel Miqne, which is located roughly eleven miles west of Jerusalem. Ashdod, located about twenty miles south of Tel Aviv, is the fifth largest city in Israel today. Gaza, located three miles from the Mediterranean coast, marks the southern border of Canaan. Ashkelon is situated on the Mediterranean coast, approximately thirty miles south of Tel Aviv. The exact location of Gath has yet to be determined.

The Philistines soon grew dissatisfied with their narrow strip of land and sought to expand their kingdom eastward. Those expansion plans coincided with those of the Israelites, who were steadily moving westward. Conflict was inevitable.

In the years leading up to the Israelite monarchy, the Philistines emerged as Israel's chief adversaries. They were also used as instruments of God's punishment from time to time. According to Judges 13:1, when the Israelites disobeyed God, he allowed the Philistines to rule over them for forty years.

While most Israelites considered the land of the Philistines enemy territory, David, the future king, actually found refuge there. On the run from King Saul, David volunteered the services of his band of warriors to Achish, the king of Philistia. In return, Achish offered David the town of Ziklag in southern Philistia (1 Samuel 27:1–12).

Saul's obsession with finding David put his kingdom at risk. While Saul and his men pursued David, the Philistines marshaled their forces against Israel. David and his men would have been part of the Philistine forces at Aphek if the other Philistine commanders hadn't opposed the idea.

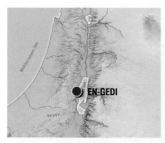

En-Gedi spring

En-Gedi Nahal, David's caves

David's Hiding Places

1 SAMUEL 18:6—29:11

David's troubles with King Saul began on the journey home after defeating the Philistine giant Goliath. As Israel's warriors passed through the streets of Gibeah, women sang out, *"Saul has killed a thousand enemies; David has killed ten thousand!"* (1 Samuel 18:7).

■ *David spent the better part of a decade on the run from Saul.*

Saul became paranoid, convinced that David was going to overthrow him and take the throne. David remained loyal to Saul, even after Saul tried more than once to kill him with a spear. With his life in danger, David became a fugitive. He moved from one location to another in and around the kingdom—always one step ahead of Saul's forces.

David's journey reads like a travelogue of Canaan. His first stop after fleeing Saul was Ramah, a town about five miles north of Jerusalem and home of the prophet Samuel. Saul got word of David's location, but when he and his men tried to apprehend David, God intervened.

David then fled to Nob, a few miles to the south, where Ahimelech the priest fed him bread used for sacrifices. He also gave David Goliath's sword as a weapon. From there, David traveled west to Gath, Goliath's hometown in Philistia. David's reputation preceded him, though, and he was regarded as a threat; so in order to escape imprisonment, David pretended to be insane.

For a while, David moved to Adullam Cave in Judah, where he was joined by 400 warriors. His next step was to ensure the safety of his father and mother. He escorted them all the way to Mizpah in Moab to shield them from Saul's vengeance. On the way back, he camped briefly on the western shore of the Dead Sea before heading northwest to Hereth Forest.

While there, David learned that Saul had killed Ahimelech in Nob for helping him. He also learned the Philistines were looting the nearby city of Keilah, so he and his men, who now numbered 600, hurried there to stop them. After securing victory over the Philistines, David learned that Saul was on his way to Keilah. David and his men fled to the Ziph Desert and then the Maon Desert.

When the desert proved to be unsafe, David and his followers moved to a remote region near the Dead Sea called En-Gedi. While there, David was given an opportunity to kill Saul and end his running. Yet he chose to spare the king's life.

David and his men headed south and then back into the Maon Desert. There David had a second opportunity to kill Saul—and again he refused. Convinced that Philistia was the only safe place for him and his men, David returned to Gath and offered his services to King Achish of the Philistines. In return, Achish gave David the city of Ziklag in southern Philistia. That was where David stayed until Saul and his son Jonathan were killed in battle with the Philistines (2 Samuel 1:1–12).

DAVID'S HIDING PLACES IN THE BIBLE

David and his 600 men got out of there fast and started moving from place to place. Saul heard that David had left Keilah, and he decided not to go after him. (1 Samuel 23:13)

Masada is a wilderness fortress; David may have hidden here or in similar hiding places.

Source of mineral water spring in Ein Gedi National Park near the Dead Sea in Israel

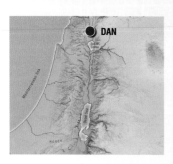

Variations of the phrase *"from Dan in the north to Beersheba in the south"* occur several times in the Old Testament. It was a description of the boundaries of Israel (see 2 Samuel 3:9–10; 17:11; 24:2, 15; 1 Kings 4:25; 2 Chronicles 30:5). Beersheba, Dan's southern counterpart, was located at the edge of the Southern (Negev) Desert. The distance from Dan to Beersheba is approximately 144 miles.

Dan

1 KINGS 12

Dan, formerly known as Laish (Judges 18:7–31), was a city on the northern border of Israel—a site identified with modern-day el-Qadi. Dan achieved the worst kind of notoriety following the death of King Solomon.

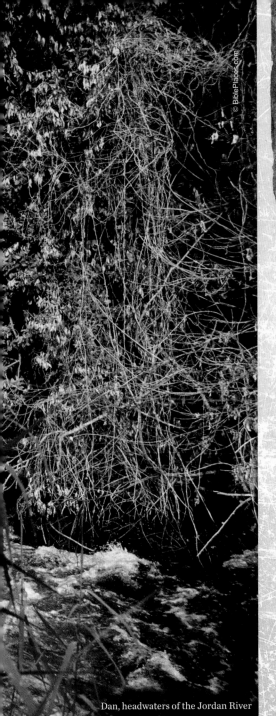

Dan, headwaters of the Jordan River

Ruler's podium with canopy structure in Dan

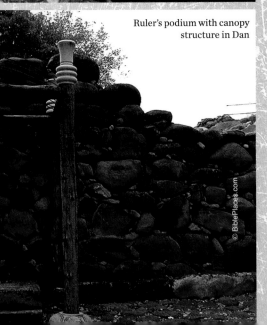

Rehoboam, Solomon's son, was the logical successor to his father. However, he alienated the people of Israel when he refused to lighten the burdens his father had imposed on them. Jeroboam, an appointee of Solomon who had rebelled against the king, saw his chance and took it.

Both Rehoboam and Jeroboam claimed the throne after Solomon's death. Most of the tribes of Israel followed Jeroboam. Only Judah followed Rehoboam, who amassed an army and prepared to reclaim the kingdom through warfare. But God stopped him. As a result, the nation was divided into two kingdoms: Israel in the north and Judah in the south.

The problem with this arrangement was that Jerusalem—the site of the temple and the center of worship for the Israelites—was located in Judah. Jeroboam feared that anyone who went to Jerusalem to worship would be persuaded to follow Rehoboam.

So Jeroboam's solution was to build worship sites in Israel—shrines that would deter his people from traveling to Jerusalem. He built one site in Bethel and one in Dan. At each, he installed a golden calf for the people to worship. From that time on, Dan was known as a center for idolatry.

Though the Israelites had struggled with idol worship throughout their history, what Jeroboam did in Dan marked a new low. Encouraging people of the Northern Kingdom to worship idols was a sure sign of God's coming judgment.

DAN IN THE BIBLE

Jeroboam asked for advice and then made two gold statues of calves. He showed them to the people and said, "Listen everyone! You won't have to go to Jerusalem to worship anymore. Here are your gods who rescued you from Egypt." Then he put one of the gold calves in the town of Bethel and the other in the town of Dan. The people sinned because they started going to these places to worship. (1 Kings 12:28–30)

Elijah wasn't the only remaining prophet of God in Israel. According to 1 Kings 18:1–15, a man named Obadiah hid 100 of God's prophets in caves until they were out of danger.

Horses in pasture on Mount Carmel

MOUNT CARMEL IN THE BIBLE

Ahab got everyone together, then they went to meet Elijah on Mount Carmel. (1 Kings 18:20)

Mount Carmel

1 KINGS 18

The northern kingdom of Israel was in dire straits. Ahab was king, Jezebel was queen, and both were evil to the core. Ahab encouraged the Israelites to worship false gods and goddesses, including Baal and Asherah, while his wife Jezebel issued an order to kill all the prophets of God.

Elijah used twelve stones for his altar, one for each of the tribes of Israel.

S uch evil could not go unpunished. God sent the prophet Elijah to warn Ahab of an impending drought. For the next three years, not a drop of rain or dew fell on Israel. Rivers dried up. Livestock died. People suffered. And Ahab blamed Elijah for the nation's troubles.

The next time the two met, Elijah delivered another message to the king—this one in the form of a challenge. He invited the king's spiritual advisors—450 prophets of Baal and 400 prophets of Asherah—to meet him on Mount Carmel for a contest to determine whose god was worth following.

In choosing Mount Carmel as the site of the showdown, Elijah offered his opponents a distinct home-field advantage. Mount Carmel was a fifteen-mile range of fertile, forested hills that stretched from the Samaritan hill country in the west all the way to the Mediterranean Sea. The effects of the drought weren't readily apparent on Mount Carmel, and many onlookers likely attributed its continued lushness to Baal.

The rules of Elijah's contest were simple. The prophets of Baal would prepare a bull for sacrifice. Elijah would do the same. The deity who acknowledged his sacrifice with fire would be named the true God of Israel.

The prophets of Baal went first. They called upon Baal to accept their sacrifice by sending fire. They begged and pleaded. They danced around their altar. They slashed themselves with swords and knives. Yet there was no response.

When Elijah's turn came, he built a stone altar and instructed bystanders to dig a trench around it. He prepared the wood and animal sacrifice—and then he did something unexpected. He asked people to fill four large jars of water and pour it over the wood and sacrifice. Then he had them do it again—and again, until the water had drenched the altar and filled the trench.

Elijah then asked God to reveal himself to the people of Israel. Immediately fire descended from heaven and consumed the offering, the wood, the stone altar, and even the water in the trench.

The people of Israel were amazed. They fell prostrate on the spot and worshiped God. Afterward, they seized the prophets of Baal and put them to death. With Israel's idol worship temporarily abated, God sent much-needed rain on the land.

THE SHOWDOWN ON **MOUNT CARMEL**

As Obadiah was walking along, he met Elijah. Obadiah recognized him, bowed down, and asked, "Elijah, is it really you?"

"Yes. Go tell Ahab I'm here."

Obadiah replied:

> *King Ahab would kill me if I told him that. And I haven't even done anything wrong. I swear to you in the name of the living Lord your God that the king has looked everywhere for you. He sent people to look in every country, and when they couldn't find you, he made the leader of each country swear that you were not in that country. Do you really want me to tell him you're here?*

> *What if the Lord's Spirit takes you away as soon as I leave? When Ahab comes to get you, he won't find you. Then he will surely kill me.*

> *I have worshiped the Lord since I was a boy. I even hid 100 of the Lord's prophets in caves when Jezebel was trying to kill them. I also gave them food and water. Do you really want me to tell Ahab you're here? He will kill me!*

Elijah said, "I'm a servant of the living Lord All-Powerful, and I swear in his name that I will meet with Ahab today."

Obadiah left and told Ahab where to find Elijah.

Ahab went to meet Elijah, and when he saw him, Ahab shouted, "There you are, the biggest troublemaker in Israel!"

Elijah answered:

> *You're the troublemaker—not me! You and your family have disobeyed the Lord's commands by worshiping Baal.*

> *Call together everyone from Israel to meet me on Mount Carmel. Be sure to bring along the 450 prophets of Baal and the 400 prophets of Asherah who eat at Jezebel's table.*

Ahab got everyone together, then they went to meet Elijah on Mount Carmel. Elijah stood in front of them and said, "How much longer will you try to have things both ways? If the Lord is God, worship him! But if Baal is God, worship him!" (1 Kings 18:7–21)

Standing on Mount Carmel overlooking Bahai Gardens in Haifa, Israel

Ancient relief of Assyrian warriors

During the later Persian occupation of Judah, exiles such as Mordecai and Esther were able to assist their fellow Jews from positions of influence within the Persian government. Esther became the queen of Persia when she married King Xerxes (Esther 2:1–18). Mordecai became a trusted royal advisor after he reported a plan to kill the king (Esther 2:19–23) and uncovered a genocidal plot against the Jews (Esther 3:1—10:3).

Ruins of the Xerxes palace (Shiraz, Iran)

Exile in Babylon

2 KINGS 24:14–16; 25:11–12

The northern kingdom of Israel fell to the Assyrians in 722 BC. The invading army deported many Israelites back to Assyria, where they spent the rest of their lives in exile.

The southern kingdom of Judah managed to maintain its independence for over 110 years after Israel fell. However, in 605 BC, a group of Judah's royal family members and elite advisors were captured and deported hundreds of miles east to Babylonia (Daniel 1:3–7). Eight years later, 10,000 more Judeans, including leading military personnel and skilled craftsmen, were sent into exile (2 Kings 24:14–16; Jeremiah 52:28–30).

The Babylonians finally conquered Judah and laid waste to Jerusalem in 586 BC. Afterward, more Judeans were deported. Others, particularly the poorest in the region, were left behind to tend to the land (2 Kings 25:11–12).

The journey from Judah to Babylonia was torturous. The route the exiles took covered 700 miles. Day after day, week after week, month after month, the people of Judah were marched north to Aleppo, and then east-southeast to Babylonia. None of them knew what lay in store. Many surely died along the way.

The prophet Jeremiah promised the exiles that the Lord would be with them and urged them to live at peace with their captors as well as they could. He reminded them of God's promise to restore them one day to the promised land (Jeremiah 24:1–10; 29:1–14).

Some captives thrived in exile by following Jeremiah's advice. Daniel and his friends Shadrach, Meshach, and Abednego became trusted advisors in the royal court of Babylon (Daniel 2:48–49).

In 539 BC, Cyrus, the king of the Persian Empire, captured Babylonia and became its monarch. He promptly emancipated the Jewish people and allowed 50,000 of them to return to their homeland (Ezra 1—2).

EXILE IN BABYLON IN THE BIBLE

Beside the rivers of Babylon we thought about Jerusalem, and we sat down and cried. (Psalm 137:1)

The Western Wall is all that remains of the temple built by Herod

The Temple in Jerusalem

1 KINGS 6; EZRA 1–8 ; HAGGAI 1–2

The Jerusalem temple served as the center of Israel's worship and national life. Its importance to Israel's identity cannot be overstated. It was, after all, the dwelling place of God.

King Solomon oversaw the construction of the first Jerusalem temple on a place called the Temple Mount—that is, Mount Moriah—in the tenth century BC. The basic shape of the building was rectangular. Scholars estimate the interior dimensions were roughly 105 feet long, 35 feet wide, and 52 feet high.

Solomon's Temple stood for centuries, until the Babylonian invasion of 586 BC. Under orders from King Nebuchadnezzar II, Babylonian forces destroyed Jerusalem and the temple. Many important Israelites were taken captive. The city and its people were reduced to mere shells of their former existences.

Around 516 BC, Jewish exiles secured permission from Zerubbabel, the governor of the region, to return to Jerusalem to rebuild and restore the temple to its former glory. This second temple, also known as Zerubbabel's Temple, served the Israelites for hundreds of years.

As control of Israel passed from Persia to Greece to Rome, the temple was sacked and desecrated repeatedly. Around 20 BC, Herod, the Roman king of Israel, negotiated an agreement with Jewish religious leaders to reconstruct Zerubbabel's Temple as an enormous, impressive temple complex—one that covered the entire Temple Mount. Workers dug a trench around Mount Moriah to support the giant walls that would surround the complex.

Though Herod's Temple is considered one of the most impressive construction projects of the first century BC, it did not last long. During a siege of Jerusalem in AD 70, Roman forces burned and destroyed the complex.

JERULSALEM

Today the Temple Mount is the site of a Muslim shrine known as the Dome of the Rock. The people of Israel are prohibited by law from worshiping there. Instead they focus their attention on the Western Wall—a remnant of the structure that surrounded the courtyard of Herod's Temple. Jewish people pray at this site today because of its proximity to the former location of the most holy place. Many write their prayers on scraps of paper and insert them into cracks in the wall.

THE TEMPLE IN JERUSALEM IN THE BIBLE

The Lord told Solomon: "If you obey my commands and do what I say, I will keep the promise I made to your father David. I will live among my people Israel in this temple you are building, and I will not desert them." So Solomon's workers finished building the temple. (1 Kings 6:11–14)

Chapter 5: THE KINGDOM OF ISRAEL

The temple was the site of several key New Testament events:

- John the Baptist's birth announcement (Luke 1:11–20)

- Jesus' boyhood visit, where he astounded teachers with his insight (Luke 2:42–52)

- Jesus' expulsion of the moneychangers (Mark 11:15–19)

- The apostle Paul's arrest (Acts 21:27–36)

Dome of the Rock and Western Wall in Jerusalem, Israel

JERUSALEM

BETHLEHEM

Introduction

The geopolitical landscape of Israel changed markedly during the time between the Old and New Testaments. The Gospel narrative begins during the final years of the BC era. Israel is an occupied land and has been for the better part of 700 years by this time.

Occupation had become a fact of life for God's people. The only thing that changed was the nationality of their oppressors. The Assyrians, Babylonians, Medes and Persians, and Greeks all took their turns ruling over Israel. In the first century BC, the Romans assumed control and absorbed Israel into their vast empire. The centuries of occupation did little to quell the Israelites' hunger for independence. Though

Rome allowed them to maintain their religious and cultural identity, the Jewish people longed to throw off the shackles of occupation altogether and become a sovereign nation once more.

They looked to Jewish prophecy for hope. The people of Israel believed that God would send someone to save them from oppression and occupation—a Messiah who would reign over a sovereign Jewish nation.

Geopolitics figured heavily in the Jewish people's messianic expectations, which reached a fever pitch during the life and ministry of Jesus. Every time a story broke about Jesus' power over nature, disease, and death, these messianic

Nabi Samuel, tomb of the prophet Samuel in the Judean Desert

Chapter 6

Judea

expectations increased. Even his disciples believed Jesus came to lead an armed revolt against Rome.

When Jesus revealed his true purpose was not to lead an uprising against the Roman occupiers, certain Jewish religious leaders and others turned against him. Their desire for a political Messiah blinded them to the much bigger revolution he offered.

The Judean geography of the New Testament is tied closely to the footsteps of Jesus. The cities of the region find their identity as settings for

prominent stature as the Savior's birthplace. Jerusalem serves as the location for his teachings in the temple and his trials before the Jewish leaders and Roman authorities.

Bethphage, a town whose precise location has never been determined, achieved a modicum of fame as the place where Jesus' disciples found the donkey and colt he used to enter Jerusalem during the final week of his earthly life.

Put simply, names such as Bethany, Gethsemane, and the Mount of Olives are famous today because of what Jesus did there.

Bethlehem

MATTHEW 2:1–12; LUKE 2:1–20

During Old Testament times, the town of Bethlehem rose to prominence as the family home of King David (1 Samuel 17:12). When David was still a young man, the prophet Samuel traveled to Bethlehem to anoint him as the future king of Israel (1 Samuel 16:4–13).

The prophet Micah elevated Bethlehem's status further with this pronouncement: *Bethlehem Ephrath, you are one of the smallest towns in the nation of Judah. But the LORD will choose one of your people to rule the nation—someone whose family goes back to ancient times* (Micah 5:2). From then on, the Jewish people looked to Bethlehem as the birthplace of the Messiah, the one who would save and rule over Israel.

If Joseph and Mary were aware of Micah's prophecy, they may have wondered why God chose them to be the earthly parents of his Son. After all, they were from the village of Nazareth (see pages 114–115). They could not foresee how God would work in and through human events to fulfill his prophecy.

The trigger event was a census, of all things. Caesar Augustus ordered every Jewish adult male to register for the census in the city of his ancestor. For Joseph, a descendant of King David, this meant a three-day trip to Bethlehem, accompanied by his fiancée Mary.

Because the town was crowded with other taxpayers, there was no room for the young couple at the local inn (or perhaps in the guest room of Joseph's ancestral home, depending on how Luke 2 is translated). The only accommodations they could find were in a shelter built for animals. So it was there in Bethlehem that Mary gave birth to the Messiah—the Son of God and Savior of the world.

At the time, Bethlehem was a small town located about five miles south of Jerusalem. Today it is a Palestinian city of about 25,000, part of the West Bank. The Church of the Nativity marks the traditional site of Jesus' birth. Commissioned by the emperor Constantine in AD 327, it is recognized as the oldest continuously operating church in the world.

BETHLEHEM
IN THE BIBLE

So Joseph had to leave Nazareth in Galilee and go to Bethlehem in Judea. Long ago Bethlehem had been King David's hometown, and Joseph went there because he was from David's family.
(Luke 2:4)

The Church of the Nativity of Jesus Christ, Bethlehem

Just outside Bethlehem to the north lies the traditional site of the tomb of Rachel, Jacob's beloved wife. Rachel died while giving birth to Benjamin, Jacob's twelfth son. The family was en route from Bethel at the time. Genesis 35:19 says, *"Rachel was buried beside the road to Ephrath, which is also called Bethlehem."*

89

Jerusalem

MATTHEW 21–23; MARK 11–13; LUKE 9:51–56; 19–21

The New Testament is largely silent about most of Jesus' early life. We know precious little about what happened to him from infancy until the start of his public ministry around thirty years of age. The rare exception is a story in Luke 2:41–52 about the twelve-year-old Jesus accompanying his parents—and many other pilgrims—to Jerusalem for the Passover Festival.

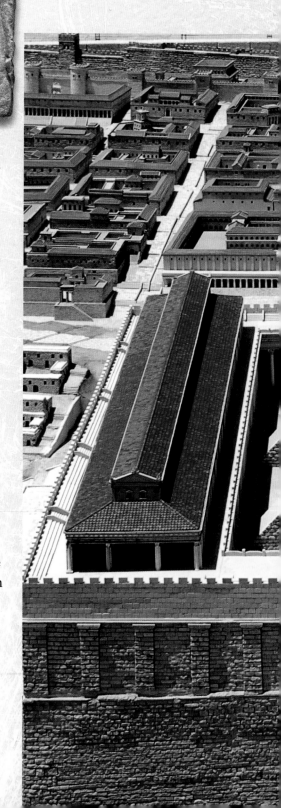

O n their way home, Joseph and Mary discovered that Jesus wasn't among their traveling party. They returned to Jerusalem and found him in the temple courts, listening to the teachers and asking them questions. The young Jesus' knowledge and understanding astounded everyone who heard him.

When Mary expressed her exasperation, Jesus simply yet profoundly replied: *"Didn't you know that I would be in my Father's house?"* (Luke 2:49b). Years later, during his public ministry, Jesus would spend quite a bit of time in his Father's house.

In the final year of his earthly ministry, Jesus returned to the temple while he was in Jerusalem for the Festival of Shelters. He began to teach and soon drew a crowd. His listeners marveled at Jesus' wisdom and wondered how he could know so much without having had a formal education.

Jesus' undeniable authority stirred up controversy among the temple officials. Some accused him of being demon-possessed. Some concluded that he was a prophet. Others acknowledged him as the Messiah and put their faith in him.

The chief priests and Pharisees, eager to limit Jesus' influence, sent the temple guards to arrest him. However, their plans did not coincide with God's timetable, so they were unable to lay a hand on Jesus (John 7:1–52).

The day after Jesus made his final entry into Jerusalem, he returned to the temple. In the courtyard of the temple, he found people selling animals for sacrifice and exchanging foreign currency for the necessary temple currency. Such business should have been done outside the temple, not inside the courtyard. Jesus overturned their tables and drove them out.

The temple Jesus knew—Herod's Temple—was actually the second temple built on that site. First completed by exiles who returned to Jerusalem around five hundred years before Jesus, the temple underwent a massive expansion project beginning around 20 BC. The renovated temple and courts were dedicated in 10 BC.

Full construction was not actually completed until AD 64, which means the temple complex was still a work in progress during Jesus' earthly ministry. The finished complex stood fully built for only six years before it was destroyed in AD 70 by the Romans.

Solomon's Porch was a public place with tall columns along the east side of the temple. The modern-day colonnade is reminiscent of the columns in Jesus' day.

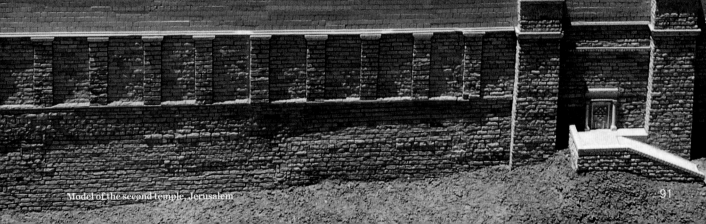

Model of the second temple, Jerusalem

A day later he returned to the temple to teach in the courtyard. His enemies turned out in force to confront him. They asked him where his authority came from. Jesus recognized their ulterior motive and turned the tables on them by asking where John the Baptist, a respected prophet, had derived his authority. When the religious leaders refused to answer, Jesus in turn refused to answer their original question.

Jesus then told a parable about two sons (Matthew 21:28–32), a parable about the renters of a vineyard (Matthew 21:33–44), and a parable about a great banquet (Matthew 22:1–14). The chief priests and Pharisees understood that they were being cast in a bad light in these parables. They considered having Jesus arrested but were afraid the temple crowd would turn on them if they did.

Tired of being the objects of scorn, the religious leaders went on the offensive. They laid a verbal trap for Jesus by asking him about paying taxes to Rome. Jesus countered with a response so brilliant that all his enemies could do was walk away (Matthew 22:15–22).

Other religious leaders tried to stir up trouble by asking him about marriage in heaven and what the greatest commandment was. Jesus again offered responses that amazed his listeners. Then he turned the tables and asked some Pharisees a tricky theological question. After that, according to Matthew 22:46b, *"no one dared ask him any more questions."*

Jesus ended his teaching that day with several devastating condemnations of the Jewish religious leaders. He called the Pharisees and teachers of the Law for the hypocrites they were.

As Jesus was walking away from the courtyard, his disciples called his attention to the impressive buildings in Herod's Temple complex. *"Jesus replied, 'Do you see these buildings? They will certainly be torn down! Not one stone will be left in place' "* (Matthew 24:2).

Jesus' prophecy proved startlingly correct. Less than forty years later, Roman forces under the command of Titus (who later became emperor of Rome) destroyed Jerusalem and tore apart the temple buildings stone by stone.

Every Jewish male twenty years of age and older was expected to pay an annual tax to finance the upkeep of the temple. The tax was equivalent to two days' wages. The question of whether Jesus would pay the tax was answered in a most unusual way. He instructed Peter to go to a nearby lake, cast his fishing line, open the mouth of the first fish he caught, and use the coin he found there to pay the tax (Matthew 17:24–27).

JERUSALEM
IN THE BIBLE

That winter, Jesus was in Jerusalem for the Temple Festival. One day he was walking in the part of the temple known as Solomon's Porch, and the people gathered all around him. They said, "How long are you going to keep us guessing? If you are the Messiah, tell us plainly!" (John 10:22–24)

Church of the Holy Sepulchre, Jerusalem

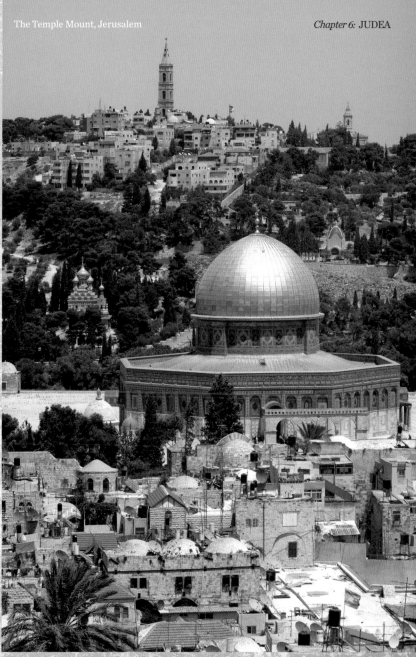

Church of the Holy Sepulchre, lighting of candles

According to Jewish tradition, Joseph and Mary brought the infant Jesus to the temple to be presented to the Lord and to offer a sacrifice. Two people at the temple—a devout man named Simeon and a prophetess named Anna—recognized the baby Jesus as the Savior (Luke 2:22–39).

The Mount of Olives

MATTHEW 24; MARK 13; LUKE 21

The Mount of Olives is the tallest of three peaks on a mountain ridge that runs across the Kidron Valley, east of the Old City of Jerusalem. The Judean Desert begins on the eastern side of the mountain. At its peak, Mount Olivet (as it is also known) rises about 230 feet above the Temple Mount in Jerusalem. The mountain is named for the olive groves that were once plentiful on its slopes.

View of Jerusalem from the Mount of Olives.

The site is first mentioned in Scripture in connection with a rebellion against King David that was initiated by David's son Absalom. Fearing for his life, David led his fighting men and members of his family out of Jerusalem and up the Mount of Olives (2 Samuel 15:13–37). At the top of the mountain he met a man named Hushai, who agreed to act as a spy for David.

The prophet Ezekiel revealed the sacred nature of the mountain in one of his visions. *"After the Lord had finished speaking, the winged creatures spread their wings and flew into the air, and the wheels were beside them. The brightness of the Lord's glory above them left Jerusalem and stopped at a hill east of the city"* (Ezekiel 11:22–23). That hill was the Mount of Olives.

The prophet Zechariah upped the ante with his apocalyptic vision of the Lord standing on the Mount of Olives and causing it to split in half from east to west. Zechariah foresaw that the wide valley created by the split would serve as an escape route for people fleeing the Lord's attack (Zechariah 14:4).

Jesus offered one of his last extended teachings to his followers on the Mount of Olives. In response to a question about how to recognize the time of his return, Jesus gave his disciples some insight into the future (Matthew 24). According to Luke 22:39–46, Jesus went to the Mount of Olives to pray prior to his arrest.

During busy times of the year—Passover, for example—travelers who could not find lodging in Jerusalem stayed on the Mount of Olives. Jesus preferred to stay in the mountain village of Bethany, where his friends Mary, Martha, and Lazarus lived.

According to Acts 1:9–13, Jesus ascended to heaven from the Mount of Olives (see pages 108–109).

THE MOUNT OF OLIVES
IN THE BIBLE

Later, as Jesus was sitting on the Mount of Olives, his disciples came to him in private and asked, "When will this happen? What will be the sign of your coming and of the end of the world?" (Matthew 24:3)

below: Mount of Olives.

The Upper Room of the Last Supper

MARK 14:12–31; LUKE 22:12

When Jesus entered Jerusalem for what turned out to be the final week of his life, his first order of business was securing a place to celebrate Passover with his disciples. Passover is one of the holiest days on the Jewish calendar, a solemn remembrance of how God spared the Hebrew firstborns during the tenth and final plague in Egypt (Exodus 12:1–30).

Jesus dispatched his most trusted disciples, Peter and John, to find a suitable location. That evening Jesus and his disciples gathered in a large upper room for their last meal together before Jesus' crucifixion. While they ate, Jesus explained in broad terms what was about to happen. He announced that one person at the table would betray him and the rest would run scared before the night was over.

When the apostle Peter objected, pledging his everlasting devotion, Jesus predicted that before the sun rose, Peter would publicly deny even knowing him—not once but three times. While the other disciples sat stunned by Jesus' news, Judas Iscariot slipped away to make plans for handing Jesus over to his enemies. The thirteen men in that room never gathered as a complete group again.

The setting for the Last Supper was a house in Jerusalem with a large upstairs room used for guests. Some scholars believe the same room was used by the disciples in Acts 1:13, in which case, this site may have become the place where the apostles stayed whenever they visited Jerusalem.

The site, known as the Cenacle, has been popular among Christian pilgrims since the fourth century AD. The history of the building now associated with the site is uncertain. Parts of the structure have been damaged, destroyed, and rebuilt countless times since then.

THE UPPER ROOM IN THE BIBLE

Jesus said to two of the disciples, "Go into the city, where you will meet a man carrying a jar of water. Follow him, and when he goes into a house, say to the owner, 'Our teacher wants to know if you have a room where he can eat the Passover meal with his disciples.' The owner will take you upstairs and show you a large room furnished and ready for you to use. Prepare the meal there." (Mark 14:13–15)

The Eucharist—the observance of Holy Communion—is based on Jesus' words and actions during the Last Supper.

During the meal Jesus took some bread in his hands. He blessed the bread and broke it. Then he gave it to his disciples and said, "Take this. It is my body." Jesus picked up a cup of wine and gave thanks to God. He gave it to his disciples, and they all drank some. Then he said, "This is my blood, which is poured out for many people, and with it God makes his agreement." (Mark 14:22–24)

Cenacle (room of the Last Supper). According to tradition, this is the site where Jesus and his disciples held the Passover feast.

The Garden of Gethsemane

MATTHEW 26:36–46; MARK 14:32–42; LUKE 22:39–46

The Last Supper ended with ten of Jesus' disciples alarmed and confused. However, one of the twelve disciples (Peter) committed to keeping Jesus from harm, and one of them (Judas Iscariot) was determined to carry out his treacherous plot. Jesus himself needed some time with his heavenly Father. He left the upper room, where the Last Supper was held, for a place where he could pour out his heart to God.

The Church of All Nations, or Basilica of the Agony, near the Garden of Gethsemane at the Mount of Olives in Jerusalem

Matthew and Mark refer to the site as Gethsemane. John identifies it as a garden. The biblical account suggests that it was somewhere across the Kidron Valley from Jerusalem on the western slope of the Mount of Olives. Some scholars identify Gethsemane with the modern-day Church of All Nations, which overlooks a garden with a stone called the Rock of the Agony.

Gethsemane was the site of some of the most intense hours of Jesus' life. He asked his most trusted disciples—Peter, James, and John—to keep watch while he prayed. This was no time of quiet reflection, though. Jesus was facing a physical, emotional, and spiritual agony unlike anything he had experienced up to now. Luke 22:44 says, *"Jesus was in great pain and prayed so sincerely that his sweat fell to the ground like drops of blood."* Jesus asked God to remove his burden from him, if at all possible, and then affirmed his commitment to carrying out God's plan.

Three times Jesus rose to check on his companions and three times he found them asleep. The third time he woke them just as a mob of his enemies was approaching—led by Judas Iscariot.

THE GARDEN OF GETHSEMANE
IN THE BIBLE

Jesus went with his disciples to a place called Gethsemane, and he told them, "Sit here while I pray." (Mark 14:32)

Peter was not about to let the mob apprehend Jesus without a fight. According to John 18:10, Peter pulled out his sword and cut off the right ear of Malchus, a servant of the high priest. He may very well have inflicted more injury if Jesus had not stopped him.

Jesus told Peter to put his sword away because the events that were about to unfold were part of God's plan. He then healed Malchus's ear (Luke 22:51).

Peter's brazen act came back to haunt him just a few hours later. Having followed Jesus and the arresting mob back to the high priest's house, Peter tried to maintain a low profile in the courtyard. According to John 18:26, a relative of Malchus recognized Peter and fingered him as one of Jesus' followers.

Olive trees in the Garden of Gethsemane

Via Dolorosa/ Stations of the Cross

The Via Dolorosa (which is Latin for "Way of Grief") is a road in the Old City of Jerusalem that traces Jesus' path from his trial before Pilate to his death on the cross. The stations of the cross are fourteen points along the way—sites where specific events occurred in the hours between Jesus' arrest and his crucifixion.

Catholics and other Christians celebrate the traditional stations of the cross and include six events not recorded anywhere in Scripture. A revised version called the Scriptural Way of the Cross was introduced by Pope John Paul II in 1991, following the biblical narrative more closely. Here are the fourteen stations of the Scriptural Way of the Cross.

1. Jesus prays in the Garden of Gethsemane.

Jesus spent the hours before his arrest praying in a garden called Gethsemane on the Mount of Olives (Matthew 26:36–46; see also pages 98–99).

2. Jesus is betrayed by Judas and arrested.

The traitorous disciple Judas Iscariot led a mob organized by the Jewish religious leaders to Gethsemane. Judas greeted Jesus with a kiss and then watched as the mob led him away (Matthew 26:47–56).

3. Jesus is condemned by the Sanhedrin.

The mob took Jesus from Gethsemane to the house of the high priest in Jerusalem. There he was put on trial by the Jewish religious leaders and found guilty of blasphemy when he refused to deny that he was the Messiah (or "Christ"), the Son of God (Matthew 26:62–68; Luke 22:66–71).

4. Jesus is denied by Peter.

The apostle Peter followed Jesus to the high priest's house but was careful to keep a safe distance. Someone in the crowd recognized Peter as being a follower of Jesus, which Peter denied. A second person recognized him, and a second time Peter denied knowing Jesus. When a third person recognized him, Peter swore he didn't know Jesus. He was devastated when he remembered that Jesus had predicted his three denials just hours earlier (Matthew 26:57–58, 69–75).

5. Jesus is judged by Pilate.

The Jewish leaders could not condemn Jesus to death. Only the Roman governor had the authority to do so. So the religious leaders took Jesus to Pilate, the Roman prefect of Judea. Pilate quickly ascertained Jesus' innocence, but when Jesus refused to defend himself, Pilate gave in to the people's demands and ordered his execution anyway (Mark 15:1–15). The Via Dolorosa begins at Pilate's hall of judgment, which may have been located in the Antonia Fortress on the northwest corner of the Temple Mount.

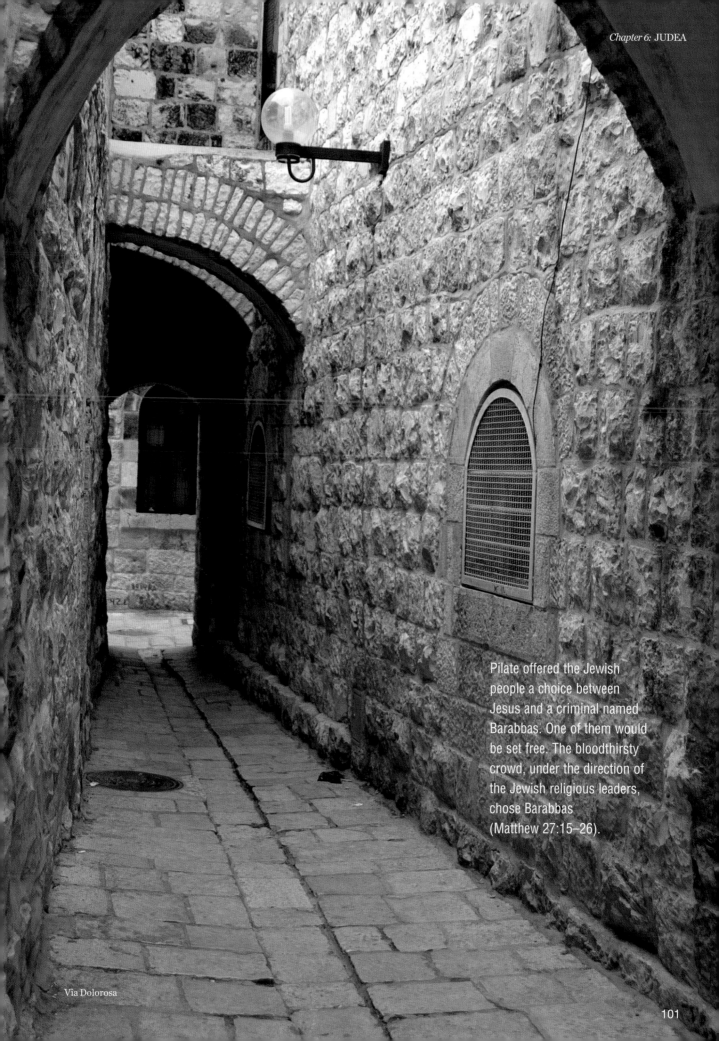

Pilate offered the Jewish people a choice between Jesus and a criminal named Barabbas. One of them would be set free. The bloodthirsty crowd, under the direction of the Jewish religious leaders, chose Barabbas (Matthew 27:15–26).

Via Dolorosa

6. Jesus is scourged and crowned with thorns.

Pilate's soldiers took Jesus to the Praetorium, the governor's official residence in Jerusalem. The soldiers stripped Jesus of his clothes and put a scarlet robe and a crown of thorns on him. They spit on him, mocked him, and beat him savagely (Matthew 27:27–30; John 19:1–3).

7. Jesus takes up his cross.

The soldiers stripped off Jesus' robe and gave him a heavy wooden cross. Jesus carried the cross from the Praetorium through the streets of Jerusalem to Golgotha (John 19:6, 15–17).

8. Jesus is helped by Simon to carry his cross.

When Jesus faltered under the weight of the cross, the Roman soldiers forced a passerby named Simon from Cyrene, a city in Libya, to help him (Mark 15:21). Today this site is marked at the corner of Via Dolorosa and El-Wad Road. From here the route turns sharply and ascends a hill via a series of stairs.

9. Jesus meets the women of Jerusalem.

A large crowd followed Jesus, including a group of women who mourned him. Jesus warned them to save their tears for themselves because of the coming judgment (Luke 23:27–31). Today this site is marked near the Church of the Holy Sepulchre.

10. Jesus is crucified.

When the procession arrived at Golgotha, the soldiers nailed Jesus' hands and feet to the cross and dropped it into place (Luke 23:33–34). Stations 10 through 14 are all marked inside the Church of the Holy Sepulchre.

11. Jesus promises his kingdom to a repentant thief.

Jesus was crucified between two criminals, one who was repentant and one who was antagonistic toward Jesus. Jesus assured the repentant criminal that his eternal future in paradise was assured (Luke 23:39–43).

12. Jesus entrusts Mary and John to each other.

Before he died, Jesus made arrangements for the care of his mother. He entrusted that task to John, his beloved disciple (John 19:25–27).

13. Jesus dies on the cross.

Around noontime, an eclipse brought darkness over the land for three hours. *"Jesus shouted, 'Father, I put myself in your hands!'"* and then gave up his life (Luke 23:44–46). This spot is marked by a Greek Orthodox crucifixion altar inside the Church of the Holy Sepulchre.

14. Jesus is laid in the tomb.

Joseph, a Jewish leader and merchant from Arimathea, asked Pilate for Jesus' body. When Pilate gave his permission, Joseph had the body wrapped in clean linen and placed in a new tomb that had been cut into a rock. He rolled a huge stone in front of the tomb (Matthew 27:57–60). A rotunda inside the Church of the Holy Sepulchre marks the spot today.

VIA DOLOROSA/ STATIONS OF THE CROSS IN THE BIBLE

Jesus was taken away, and he carried his cross to a place known as "The Skull." In Aramaic this place is called "Golgotha." (John 19:16b–17)

Jesus' Crucifixion and Burial Site

MATTHEW 27; MARK 15; LUKE 23; JOHN 19

Where was Jesus crucified? Where was his body entombed for those three days? For Christians who make the pilgrimage to the Holy Land, such questions are vital.

The Bible offers several clues from which to work. According to John 19:20, the site of the crucifixion was outside the city gate, but close to the city. John 19:41 tells us there was a garden with a tomb at the place where Jesus was crucified. Matthew 27:33 refers to the site as *"Golgotha, which means 'Place of a Skull.' "* Some scholars have suggested that the passage refers to a skull-like physical feature of the land. A more widely held theory suggests the site was notorious for executions—hence the name.

Matthew 27:39 places the site near a road where people traveled from the city to the country. Matthew 27:55 indicates that the location made it possible for people to watch from a distance, which suggests it may have been elevated. Priests were able to witness the crucifixion without worrying about being defiled by coming into contact with a dying person (Matthew 27:41; see Leviticus 21:1–4).

Despite these and other clues, scholars have yet to reach a consensus on the exact site of the crucifixion. After the Roman emperor Constantine converted to Christianity in the fourth century AD, he sent his mother Helena to the Holy Land to identify the places connected with Jesus' life.

A pagan temple stood on the traditional site of Jesus' crucifixion and resurrection. Helena ordered the temple to be torn down and a Christian church to be built in its place. Around 326 the Church of the Holy Sepulchre was consecrated. Since that time, the church has been damaged, destroyed, and reconstructed.

Today the church, also known as the Basilica of the Holy Sepulchre and the Church of the Resurrection, serves as headquarters of the Greek Orthodox Patriarch of Jerusalem.

JESUS' CRUCIFIXION AND BURIAL SITE
IN THE BIBLE

Then Joseph put the body in his own tomb that had been cut into solid rock and had never been used. He rolled a big stone against the entrance to the tomb and went away. (Matthew 27:60)

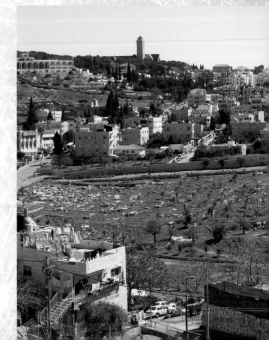

According to Matthew 27:52–53, at the moment of Jesus' death on the cross, an earthquake shook the tombs of several righteous people. The tombs broke open and the dead came back to life. After Jesus' resurrection, they went into Jerusalem and appeared to many people.

Gordon's Calvary

Post-Resurrection Appearances of Jesus

MATTHEW 28:1–20; MARK 16:1–18; LUKE 24:1–49; JOHN 20:1—21:25

The New Testament writer Luke offers a succinct description of Jesus' earthly activities after he shook off his grave clothes on Resurrection Sunday. *"For 40 days after Jesus had suffered and died, he proved in many ways that he had been raised from death. He appeared to his apostles and spoke to them about God's kingdom"* (Acts 1:3).

Those appearances began at the site that was intended to be Jesus' eternal resting place—the tomb of Joseph of Arimathea. The traditional location of the tomb is identified with the Church of the Holy Sepulchre in Jerusalem. Several tombs dating from the first century AD are preserved inside the church. Many scholars believe Jesus' tomb is among them.

Two days after Jesus' crucifixion, early on a Sunday morning, Mary Magdalene and Mary the wife of Cleopas visited Jesus' burial site. The huge stone in front of the tomb had been rolled away. On it sat an angel, who first broke the news: Jesus had risen. He was alive! As the women rushed to alert the disciples, Jesus himself appeared to them. He instructed the women to tell his disciples that they would see him in Galilee.

Later that day Jesus appeared to two of his followers on the road to Emmaus, a village about seven miles west of Jerusalem. Though he talked with them at length about spiritual things, they failed to recognize him. When they finally did, he disappeared from their midst.

That day he also appeared to ten of his disciples in the upper room of the house in Jerusalem where they had shared the Last Supper. Missing were Judas Iscariot, who had committed suicide shortly after betraying Jesus, and Thomas. Jesus ate with the men to prove that he was not a ghost.

A week later he appeared again in the upper room for the benefit of Thomas, who had doubted his fellow disciples' encounter with the risen Christ. Jesus invited Thomas to touch his scars from the crucifixion. After seeing Jesus, Thomas doubted no more.

According to 1 Corinthians 15:5–7, Jesus appeared to Peter, to James, and to a gathering of 500 followers, although no further details of these encounters are given.

In the weeks that followed, Jesus appeared to seven of his disciples who were fishing on the Sea of Galilee. On the shore afterward, he restored his relationship with Peter, who, on the night of Jesus' arrest, had denied knowing him—three times. Jesus appeared to all eleven disciples on the Mount of Olives in Galilee. (Matthew 28:16)

Ruins in Emmaus

POST-RESURRECTION APPEARANCES OF JESUS IN THE BIBLE

Suddenly Jesus met them and greeted them. They went near him, held on to his feet, and worshiped him.
(Matthew 28:9)

Several years after Jesus ascended to heaven, he appeared to a man named Saul. Saul was a staunch opponent of the early Christian movement. In fact, he helped persecute Christians and was present at the stoning of Stephen, the first recorded Christian martyr.

Saul was traveling to Damascus, an important city in the Roman province of Syria, to arrest any Christians he could find there. As he neared the city, a light from heaven knocked him to the ground. A voice called, *"Saul! Saul! Why are you so cruel to me?"*

"Who are you?" Saul asked.

"I am Jesus," came the reply.

Saul was temporarily blinded and forever changed. He stopped persecuting Christians and became one of their greatest advocates. He changed his name to Paul, helped spread the gospel throughout the Roman Empire, and penned many of the books in the New Testament (Acts 9:1–31).

Garden Tomb in Jerusalem, one of two sites proposed as the place of Jesus' burial

The Ascension of Christ

ACTS 1

Forty days after Jesus rose from the dead, he gathered his disciples on the Mount of Olives, just east of the Old City of Jerusalem. (Luke 24:50 puts the site near the town of Bethany.) Jesus lifted his hands and blessed his disciples. He charged them to be his witnesses *"in Jerusalem, in all Judea, in Samaria, and everywhere in the world"* (Acts 1:8). After he had finished speaking, he ascended to heaven.

Jesus' earthly ministry was complete.

Today the Chapel of the Ascension occupies the site traditionally associated with Jesus' dramatic return to heaven. Located on the Mount of Olives in the at-Tur district of Jerusalem, the chapel serves as a shrine to the ascension. In the floor of the chapel is a slab of stone that, according to tradition, is marked with the right footprint of Jesus.

For over 3,000 years, the Mount of Olives has been used as a Jewish cemetery. More than 150,000 graves have been dug there. The southern ridge of the mount, near the modern-day village of Silwad, is the final resting place of some of Jerusalem's most noteworthy citizens who lived during the time of the kings. According to tradition, the tombs of the prophet Zechariah and King David's rebellious son Absalom are located on the southern ridge. The traditional burial places of the prophets Haggai and Malachi can be found on the upper slope.

The popularity of the mount as a burial site is tied to the prophet Zechariah's apocalyptic vision of the Lord standing on the mountain and splitting it in half (Zechariah 14:4). Jewish tradition holds that when the long-awaited Messiah comes, the dead buried on the Mount of Olives will be raised first.

According to Acts 1:10–11, the disciples stood staring intently at the sky after Jesus was no longer visible. *"Two men dressed in white clothes"*—a common biblical description of angels—appeared beside them to ask why they were still craning their necks skyward. They told the disciples: *"Jesus has been taken to heaven. But he will come back in the same way you have seen him go."*

Dome of the Ascension

THE ASCENSION OF CHRIST
IN THE BIBLE

After Jesus had said this and while they were watching, he was taken up into a cloud. They could not see him, but as he went up, they kept looking up into the sky.

(Acts 1:9–10)

Dome of the Ascension footprint

GALILEE

Introduction

The region of Galilee was relatively small, stretching a mere forty-five miles from its northern border to its southern border. Roughly 200 villages dotted its landscape in biblical times.

Yet from this humble, nondescript region, the world was changed forever. Jesus grew up in the small Galilean village of Nazareth. He preached in the synagogue there (Luke 4:16). He chose another Galilean village, Capernaum, as his base of operations.

In Cana, Jesus changed water to wine (John 2:1–11). In Bethsaida, he fed thousands with a meager food supply (Matthew 14:13–21)

raised Jairus's daughter from the dead (Luke 8:40–56), and healed the sick and the disabled. Jesus delivered some of his best-known parables and teachings—including the Sermon on the Mount—in Galilee.

Jesus' enemies tried to use his Galilean background against him. After Jesus spoke at the temple in Jerusalem, the chief priests and Pharisees upbraided the temple guards for not arresting him. When Nicodemus, one of their own, came to Jesus' defense, his fellow religious leaders turned on him: *"Nicodemus, you must be from Galilee! Read the Scriptures, and you will find that no prophet is to come from Galilee"*

Galilee

They were wrong. According to 2 Kings 14:25, the prophet Jonah came from Galilee. Yet their ignorance of their own prophetic tradition was not the main issue. They were placing an arbitrary limit on God's ability to work. He can—and did—call prophets from a variety of backgrounds and points of origin. The homeland does not bestow honor on a prophet; the prophet bestows honor on his or her homeland.

Jesus' Galilean ministry is yet another example of how he defied human expectations at every turn. People assumed they would recognize the Messiah when he came, based on their preconceived notions of his place of origin, what he should look like, and what he should say. Yet

there were people who chose not to acknowledge Jesus as the Messiah, while others viewed him as fulfilling the messianic prophecies in the Old Testament.

Isaiah 53:2b says this about God's Chosen One: *"He wasn't some handsome king. Nothing about the way he looked made him attractive to us."* Yet those who looked past Jesus' appearance and his Galilean upbringing found the Savior they were looking for.

The Jordan River

MATTHEW 3:1–17; MARK 1:1–11; LUKE 3:1–22; JOHN 1:19–34

The New Testament Gospels are virtually silent about Jesus' life from infancy until he was about thirty years old. (The lone exception is a story in Luke 2:41–52 about Jesus' visit to the temple in Jerusalem when he was twelve.) That silence is broken by Jesus' sudden appearance at the Jordan River while John the Baptist was ministering there.

Jesus Christ being baptized by John the Baptist. From the ancient Byzantine baptistry ceiling in Ravenna, Italy.

John had attracted a large following and was baptizing people in the river. Baptism served as a public expression of repentance—a radical change in a person's life. The practice was common among Gentile converts to Judaism.

When Jesus arrived, John was understandably reluctant to baptize him. He recognized Jesus for who he was and realized that their roles should have been reversed. Yet John was open to God's will. Despite his feelings of unworthiness, John baptized Jesus as requested.

Because Jesus was sinless, he had no need to repent. Instead, his baptism demonstrated that he had been anointed by God to fulfill the role of the Messiah. It also served as an example to his followers.

John 1:28 identifies the site of Jesus' baptism as *"east of the Jordan River in Bethany."* Scholars have yet to determine conclusively the location of this site, which shared a name with the village of Bethany that is near Jerusalem.

The traditional site of Jesus' baptism is about five miles north of the Dead Sea, across the river from Jericho. Alternately, some scholars place the site a little north of the halfway point between Lake Galilee and the Dead Sea, near the site of Tell Shalem.

THE JORDAN RIVER IN THE BIBLE

From Jerusalem and all Judea and from the Jordan River Valley crowds of people went to John. They told how sorry they were for their sins, and he baptized them in the river. (Matthew 3:5–6)

About that time Jesus came from Nazareth in Galilee, and John baptized him in the Jordan River. As soon as Jesus came out of the water, he saw the sky open and the Holy Spirit coming down to him like a dove. A voice from heaven said, "You are my own dear Son, and I am pleased with you." (Mark 1:9–11).

■ *John the Baptist's words predicting that Jesus would baptize people with the Holy Spirit (Matthew 3:11) likely anticipated Jesus' sending of the Holy Spirit on the day of Pentecost (see Acts 2 for details).*

The Jordan River is mentioned in the Old Testament as a boundary or geographical feature delineating the land. For example, God described the boundaries of the promised land this way: *"The eastern border will begin at Hazar-Enan in the north, then run south to Shepham, and on down to Riblah on the east side of Ain. From there, it will go south to the eastern hills of Lake Galilee, then follow the Jordan River down to the north end of the Dead Sea"* (Numbers 34:10–12).

Nazareth

MATTHEW 2:19–23

Nazareth's reputation in first-century Israel is best illustrated by the words of the soon-to-be disciple Nathanael. When he learned that Jesus, the new rabbi his friend Philip wanted him to meet, hailed from there, he asked, *"Can anything good come from Nazareth?"* (John 1:46).

E ven Nazareth's proximity to the Via Maris, a major trade route connecting Egypt with the Mesopotamian region to the east, did little to elevate the agricultural village in Lower Galilee from its insignificant status. During Jesus' time, Nazareth had a population of 1,600 to 2,000 people.

The Old Testament contains no mention of Nazareth. The New Testament offers no information about it beyond its association with Jesus. Because the New Testament is largely silent about Jesus' life from the time he was an infant until he was about thirty years old, we may assume that Jesus spent most of his formative years in or around Nazareth.

About a year into his public ministry, Jesus returned to Nazareth to teach in the synagogue. The power of his words amazed and disturbed his listeners. *"They kept on asking, 'Isn't he Joseph's son?'"* (Luke 4:22b). The people of Nazareth had seen Jesus grow up as one of them. When Jesus hinted at his plan to reach out to Gentiles (non-Jews), his former neighbors were outraged. They grabbed him and carried him to a cliff at the edge of the village, meaning to throw him off. Jesus, however, slipped away from them unharmed.

Today Nazareth is home to the Church of the Annunciation, the largest church building in the Middle East, which commemorates the angel Gabriel's announcement of Christ's birth to the Virgin Mary. The church was built over the remains of older structures that date to AD 356.

The Nazarenes' familiarity with Jesus and his family bred a contempt that ultimately prevented them from reaping the benefits of Jesus' ministry. According to Mark 6:4–5, *"Jesus said, 'Prophets are honored by everyone, except the people of their hometown and their relatives and their own family.' Jesus could not work any miracles there, except to heal a few sick people by placing his hands on them."*

NAZARETH
IN THE BIBLE

Joseph got up and left with them for Israel. But when he heard that Herod's son Archelaus was now ruler of Judea, he was afraid to go there. Then in a dream he was told to go to Galilee, and they went to live there in the town of Nazareth. So the Lord's promise came true, just as the prophet had said, "He will be called a Nazarene." (Matthew 2:21–23)

Church of the Annunciation. This church was built on the site where, according to tradition, the Annunciation took place in Nazareth, Israel.

NAZARETH

Sheep grazing near Nazareth

© BiblePlaces.com

■ *The prophecy cited in Matthew 2:23—"He will be called a Nazarene"—is not found in the Old Testament. Scholars have yet to determine its source.*

Lake Galilee

MARK 1:14–20; LUKE 5:1–11

When the time came to select his disciples, Jesus could have gone to Jerusalem. Jesus would have had his pick of the religious cream of the crop from among the various leaders who gathered in the temple. He could have surrounded himself with twelve pillars of the community.

Instead Jesus went to Lake Galilee (also known as the Sea of Galilee), a body of fresh water in northern Palestine. The Jordan River flows into the lake from the north and out of it from the south. Though it is only about thirty-two miles in circumference, Lake Galilee is one of the major geographical features of the modern state of Israel.

The area around Lake Galilee was home to a variety of working-class people. Farmers and fruit growers were drawn to its hospitable climate, fertile soil, and abundance of water. Fishermen were drawn by the thirty-five different species of fish that inhabited the lake.

Lake Galilee

The lake's geographical location made it susceptible to abrupt changes in temperature, which caused frequent violent storms. The men who fished the lake were accustomed to danger—and, generally speaking, were a little rough around the edges themselves. Early in his ministry, Jesus encountered four such men: Simon Peter, Andrew, James, and John.

"Jesus said to them, 'Follow me! I will teach you how to bring in people instead of fish'" (Mark 1:17). All four men immediately dropped everything to follow him—and in time became Jesus' most trusted friends.

■ *What's in a name? In some Bible translations, Lake Galilee is called the Sea of Galilee. In the Old Testament, it is called Lake Chinnereth or the Sea of Chinnereth in some translations. Luke refers to it as Lake Gennesaret (Luke 5:1). In John's Gospel, it's called Lake Tiberias. Today it is known as Kinneret, the Hebrew word for "harp," in reference to its shape.*

LAKE GALILEE

LAKE GALILEE
IN THE BIBLE

As Jesus was walking along the shore of Lake Galilee, he saw Simon and his brother Andrew. They were fishermen and were casting their nets into the lake. Jesus said to them, "Follow me! I will teach you how to bring in people instead of fish." Right then the two brothers dropped their nets and went with him. Jesus walked on and soon saw James and John, the sons of Zebedee. They were in a boat, mending their nets. At once Jesus asked them to come with him. They left their father in the boat with the hired workers and went with him.
(Mark 1:16–20)

Capernaum

MATTHEW 4:12–17; MARK 1:21–2:12

Jesus chose Capernaum to serve as the base for his ministry in Galilee. Capernaum was a town on the northwest shore of Lake Galilee, less than three miles from the mouth of the Jordan River.

CAPERNAUM IN THE BIBLE

Jesus and his disciples went to the town of Capernaum. Then on the next Sabbath he went into the synagogue and started teaching. (Mark 1:21)

The Bible doesn't explain why Jesus chose Capernaum as his headquarters. Its distance from Jerusalem—over one hundred miles—may have played a role. Capernaum was close enough to allow for travel to the temple during religious festivals, yet far enough away to allow Jesus space to grow his ministry away from the spotlight of the religious establishment in Jerusalem.

Capernaum was home to five of Jesus' disciples: Peter, Andrew, James, John, and Matthew. Peter's house later served as a worship center for first-century Christians. The remains of a church from the fifth century AD occupy the traditional site of the house.

Capernaum was the site of several miraculous healings performed by Jesus:

- Peter's mother-in-law (Matthew 8:14–15)
- an army officer's servant (Matthew 8:5–13)
- a paralyzed man who was lowered through a hole in a roof (Mark 2:1–12)
- a nobleman's son (John 4:46–54)
- two blind men (Matthew 9:27–31)
- a man who could not speak (Matthew 9:32–34)

Capernaum is also where Jesus raised Jairus's daughter from the dead (Matthew 9:18–26) and told Peter to find money inside a fish's mouth that he could use to pay the temple tax (Matthew 17:24–27). Despite Jesus' miracles and teachings, however, the people of Capernaum had difficulty believing in him.

Perhaps the most telling story of Jesus' troubled relationship with the town is found in Mark 1:21–28. One Sabbath day, Jesus went to the synagogue to teach. A man possessed by an evil spirit suddenly burst in and shouted, *"Jesus from Nazareth, what do you want with us? Have you come to destroy us? I know who you are! You are God's Holy One."*

With this statement, a demon recognized Jesus for who he was. Like the people from the neighboring villages of Chorazin and Bethsaida, those living in Capernaum rejected Jesus' calls for repentance and faced his rebuke as a result.

Some scholars think Jesus' choice of Capernaum as his base of operations fulfilled a prophecy made in Isaiah 9:1b: *"The territories of Zebulun and Naphtali in Galilee were once hated. But this land of the Gentiles across the Jordan River and along the Mediterranean Sea will be greatly respected."* Capernaum was located near these territories. Respect came from the fact that the Messiah, God's own Son, chose to live there.

CAPERNAUM

above: Excavations of the ancient city of Capernaum on the shores of Lake Kinneret, where Christ lived and preached

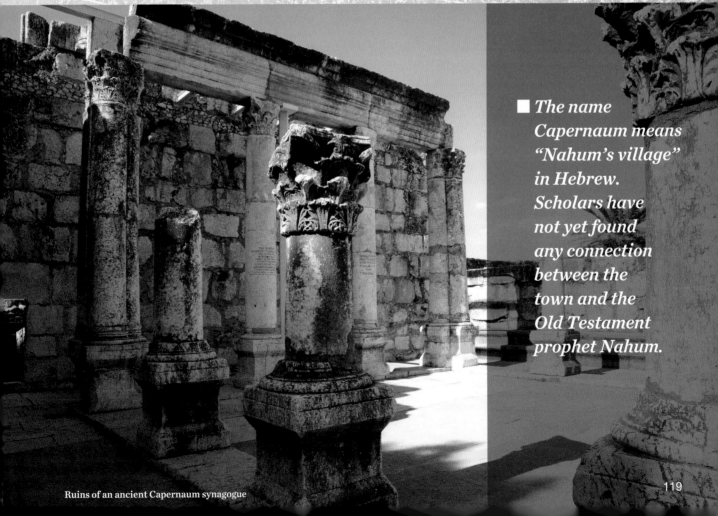

■ *The name Capernaum means "Nahum's village" in Hebrew. Scholars have not yet found any connection between the town and the Old Testament prophet Nahum.*

Ruins of an ancient Capernaum synagogue

119

Bethsaida, "house of fisherman"
© BiblePlaces.com

Bethsaida

MARK 8:22–26; LUKE 9:10–17

Bethsaida was a village closely associated with Capernaum and Chorazin during Jesus' earthly ministry. The exact location of the city is unknown, although many scholars place it near the northern shore of Lake Galilee, on the eastern side of the Jordan River. The flat northeastern shoreline of Lake Galilee is known as the Plain of Bethsaida. The name *Bethsaida* means "house of the fisherman."

Bethsaida was the hometown of three of Jesus' disciples: Philip, Andrew, and Simon Peter (John 1:44; 12:21). Philip continued to make his home there even after Jesus called him to be a disciple.

Bethsaida's remote location led to one of the most memorable miracles in Scripture. Jesus had retreated to Bethsaida for some quiet time with his disciples. When people discovered where he was, though, they came in swarms. Jesus welcomed them, healing those who were suffering and teaching about the kingdom of God.

As the hour grew late, the disciples urged Jesus to dismiss the crowd so everyone could find food and accommodations in surrounding villages. Instead, Jesus used the food they had on hand—five loaves of bread and two fish—to feed the entire crowd. He divided their meager supplies into individual portions—enough to feed 5,000 men, not counting women and children (see Matthew 14:13–21; Mark 6:30–44; Luke 9:10–17; John 6:1–14). Later Jesus healed a blind man outside Bethsaida by putting spit in his eyes (Mark 8:22–26).

Despite having a front-row seat to Jesus' miracles and teachings, the people of Bethsaida were reluctant to embrace his message. Jesus rebuked them, along with the people of Capernaum and Chorazin, for their refusal to repent and warned them of God's impending judgment (Matthew 11:20–24).

Plain of Bethsaida
© BiblePlaces.com

BETHSAIDA IN THE BIBLE

The apostles came back and told Jesus everything they had done. He then took them with him to the village of Bethsaida, where they could be alone. (Luke 9:10)

■ *Jesus' feeding of the 5,000 in Bethsaida is the only miracle that is mentioned in all four Gospels.*

BETHSAIDA

Plain of Bethsaida from northwest

© BiblePlaces.com

Identified by name seven times in the Gospels, Bethsaida is one of the most frequently referenced sites in the New Testament.

The Mount of Beatitudes

MATTHEW 5–7

Very early in his public ministry, Jesus led his disciples up the side of a hill where *"he taught them"* (Matthew 5:2). From that spot, Jesus ushered in a new way of understanding the world and our place in it.

K nown collectively as the Sermon on the Mount, Jesus' words fill three chapters of Matthew's Gospel. Though Jesus had preached in public before (Matthew 4:12–17) and had even performed miracles (Matthew 4:23–25), in this sermon he laid the groundwork for the rest of his ministry.

The Bible doesn't identify the exact place where Jesus taught, beyond referring to it as *"the side of a mountain"* (Matthew 5:1). Tradition holds that it was Mount Eremos, which is located between Tabgha and Capernaum. The site overlooks the Plain of Gennesaret, a region known for its fertility. Today a Byzantine church sits at the bottom of the mountain and a Roman Catholic Franciscan chapel sits at the top.

Identifying the precise location of Jesus' sermon, though, is much less important than understanding what occurred there. From the Mount of Beatitudes—named for the nine *"God blesses"* pronouncements that begin the Sermon on the Mount—Jesus turned conventional wisdom on its head. He reordered priorities. He set standards for his followers that brought to life the spirit of even the most stringent requirements of the Old Testament Law. To be more specific, he set standards for his followers that were impossible to meet apart from relying on his power.

Jesus' interpretation of the law—in the form of his teachings in the Sermon on the Mount—adds new meaning to the law given to Moses on Mount Sinai.

THE MOUNT OF BEATITUDES

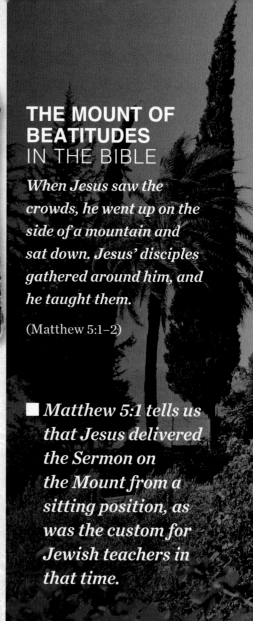

THE MOUNT OF BEATITUDES IN THE BIBLE

When Jesus saw the crowds, he went up on the side of a mountain and sat down. Jesus' disciples gathered around him, and he taught them.

(Matthew 5:1–2)

■ *Matthew 5:1 tells us that Jesus delivered the Sermon on the Mount from a sitting position, as was the custom for Jewish teachers in that time.*

The Roman Catholic chapel at the Mount of Beatitudes

© BiblePlaces.com

Caesarea Philippi

MATTHEW 16:13–20; MARK 8:27–30; LUKE 9:18–21

Caesarea Philippi was located north of Lake Galilee on the southern slope of Mount Hermon. The town was known for its shrine to Pan, the Greco-Roman god of nature. In fact, the site's original name was Paneas (or Banias). The emperor Caesar Augustus gave the city to Herod the Great, the Roman-appointed king of the Jews. When Herod's son Philip rose to power, he rebuilt the city and named it in honor of Caesar and himself.

Sacred niches at Caesarea Philipi

Caesarea Philippi is noteworthy in Christian history as the site of Peter's great realization. Jesus was about to start his final journey to Jerusalem, where he would be crucified and resurrected. His extraordinary exchange with Peter began with a simple question to all his disciples: *"What do people say about me?"* (Luke 9:18b).

At that point in his ministry, Jesus was being followed by sizable crowds—people with different views and expectations of him. Jesus was taking their pulse, checking to see what the popular theories of the moment were.

The disciples answered, *"Some people say you are John the Baptist or maybe Elijah or Jeremiah or some other prophet"* (Matthew 16:14).

Then Jesus got personal with his disciples. *"But who do you say I am?"* (Matthew 16:15).

Peter's reply is stunning in its boldness and insight: *"You are the Messiah, the Son of the living God"* (Matthew 16:16).

In response, Jesus did several things:

- He affirmed Peter's answer and identified himself as the Christ, the Messiah, the Son of God.
- He told Peter that God himself had given Peter special insight.
- He revealed his plans to use Peter as a leader in the church that was to come.
- He urged his disciples not to publicize his messianic identity.
- He continued on with his journey to Jerusalem.

CAESAREA PHILIPPI IN THE BIBLE

Jesus and his disciples went to the villages near the town of Caesarea Philippi. As they were walking along, he asked them, "What do people say about me?" (Mark 8:27)

Jesus' instruction to Peter to keep quiet about his confession should not be interpreted as a sign of reluctance or fear. Most Jewish people in the first century didn't fully understand the Messiah's role. They believed he would be a political figure who would lead them in violent revolt against Rome.

Jesus knew that claiming the title *Messiah* would confuse people and encourage the wrong expectations. Having to address their misconceptions over and over again would have been detrimental to the final days of his ministry.

■ Caesarea Philippi lies close to the *"land of the Gentiles across the Jordan River and along the Mediterranean Sea"* mentioned by the Old Testament prophet Isaiah (Isaiah 9:1).

CAESAREA PHILIPPI

© BiblePlaces.com

© BiblePlaces.com

© BiblePlaces.com

Chorazin

MATTHEW 11:20–24; LUKE 10:13–15

Chorazin was a village in northern Galilee situated on a hill overlooking the northern shore of Lake Galilee. The village was located about two miles north of Capernaum. Today the site is an excavated ruin near Karraza, Khirbat, a Palestinian Arab village in the District of Safed. Archaeologists believe Chorazin was built on a series of basalt stone terraces and covered an area of about twelve acres.

Chorazin, along with Bethsaida and Capernaum, gained notoriety in the New Testament for the stubborn refusal of its people to put their faith in Jesus, even after he performed countless signs and wonders among them. Jesus pointed out that even the Gentiles of Tyre and Sidon would have recognized the truth of his message—something the people of Chorazin failed to do. He then warned that the Gentiles of Tyre and Sidon would fare better in God's coming judgment than the people of Chorazin.

Jesus' reference to Sodom in Matthew 11:24 is chilling. Genesis 19 records the story of Sodom's wickedness and destruction. God rained sulfur down on the city, killing everyone who lived there. There is no evidence that Chorazin suffered a similar fate. However, Jesus warned that its people would face spiritual judgment and destruction for their refusal to repent and turn to God.

CHORAZIN IN THE BIBLE

In the towns where Jesus had worked most of his miracles, the people refused to turn to God. So Jesus was upset with them and said: "You people of Chorazin are in for trouble! You people of Bethsaida are in for trouble too! If the miracles that took place here had happened in Tyre and Sidon, the people there would have turned to God long ago. They would have dressed in sackcloth and put ashes on their heads. I tell you on the day of judgment the people of Tyre and Sidon will get off easier than you will."
(Matthew 11:20–22)

■ *Unlike Bethsaida and Capernaum, which were also called out by Jesus, Chorazin is mentioned nowhere else in Scripture apart from the two references to this story in Matthew 11 and Luke 10.*

127

Introduction

"From John to the seven churches in Asia."

With that salutation, John (traditionally believed to be Jesus' beloved disciple) began describing the visions and words given to him by an angel of God. The apocalyptic writings of Revelation, the last book of the Bible, were addressed to seven churches in the Roman province of Asia.

Not to be confused with the continent, Roman Asia was located in what is now western Turkey. The districts that made up this province were former Seleucid kingdoms whose rulers were known as "the kings of Asia." When King

Attalus III died without an heir, he willed his kingdom to Rome. From that point on, the province was known as Asia.

The fact that Christian churches existed in Asia is a testament to the fearlessness and diligence of Jesus' disciples. In his Great Commission (Matthew 28:19–20), Jesus instructed his followers to make disciples of all nations. Those followers took his words to heart.

Led by the Holy Spirit and equipped with the teachings of Christ they'd heard firsthand, the earliest Christians took their faith on the road—

Asia Minor

and on the sea. They set a course for relatively distant places with names such as Thyatira, Laodicea, and Colossae. When they arrived in each of their destinations, they told anyone who would listen what Jesus had done.

Certainly the most prominent of these evangelists was the apostle Paul, who spent time in the city of Ephesus during his second and third missionary journeys. Yet countless other believers—men and women whose names are lost to history but not to God—were just as instrumental in introducing Christianity to Asia Minor.

In each city they visited, Jesus' followers found a receptive audience. When that audience had grown to a modest size, a church was started. Some followers stayed in the city to lead the fledgling congregation; others moved on to plant new churches.

Where there was opportunity, though, there was also danger. The growth of Christianity in Asia Minor coincided with the rise of emperor worship throughout the Roman Empire. By law, Jews were exempt from emperor worship; Jewish Christians were not. In spreading the gospel, Jesus' followers risked persecution and death.

Facade of ancient Celsus Library in Ephesus, Turkey

EPHESUS IN THE BIBLE

This is what you must write to the angel of the church in Ephesus:

I am the one who holds the seven stars in my right hand, and I walk among the seven gold lampstands. Listen to what I say.

I know everything you have done, including your hard work and how you have endured. I know you won't put up with anyone who is evil. When some people pretended to be apostles, you tested them and found out they were liars. You have endured and gone through hard times because of me, yet you have not given up.

But I do have something against you! And it is this: You don't have as much love as you used to. Think about where you have fallen from, and then turn back and do as you did at first. If you don't turn back, I will come and take away your lampstand. But there is one thing you are doing right. You hate what the Nicolaitans are doing, and so do I.

If you have ears, listen to what the Spirit says to the churches. I will let everyone who wins the victory eat from the life-giving tree in God's wonderful garden. (Revelation 2:1–7)

Ephesus

REVELATION 2:1–7

Ephesus, one of the most important cities in the Roman Empire, was located on the Aegean coast, in the Lydia region of Asia Minor. The city lay approximately one hundred miles east of Laodicea and thirty-seven miles south of Smyrna.

Ephesus was positioned at the intersection of several major trade routes, which helped it become a key commercial center of Asia Minor. The temple of Artemis, one of the Seven Wonders of the Ancient World, was constructed there. The city's leaders curried favor with Rome by dedicating other temples and monuments to Roman leaders.

The apostle Paul stopped in Ephesus on his return from his second missionary journey (Acts 18:19–21) through Asia Minor and Macedonia. He returned to Ephesus during his third missionary journey. According to Acts 19, Paul proclaimed the good news about Jesus in the Jewish synagogue and in the lecture hall of Tyrannus. Many listeners opposed Paul and his message, but he continued to preach the gospel faithfully and ended up staying in Ephesus for almost three years before returning to Jerusalem.

Years later, during his first imprisonment in Rome (AD 61–63), Paul wrote a letter that, according to tradition, was addressed to the believers in Ephesus. In his letter, Paul explained God's goals for the church and how to fulfill them. After his release, Paul wrote a letter to Timothy, a young pastor in Ephesus. Both letters are part of the New Testament.

In the book of Revelation, John was instructed to encourage the Ephesian believers to maintain their perseverance and endurance in the face of rampant idol worship and persecution. He also instructed the church to reject the false teachings of a group called the Nicolaitans, about whom little is known.

Prior to the apostle Paul's return to Ephesus (Acts 18:21; 19:1), another Jewish convert spoke boldly about the Lord in the synagogue at Ephesus. According to Acts 18:25, Apollos, who would later become a traveling companion of Paul, "knew much about the Lord's Way, and he spoke about it with great excitement." For all his bold talk, though, Apollos was limited in his knowledge. He understood only the baptism of John (the Baptist). Two other Christians in Ephesus, Aquila and Priscilla, helped Apollos deepen his understanding of Christ.

EPHESUS

Smyrna

REVELATION 2:8–11

Smyrna was a major port city on the west coast of Asia Minor. Situated near where the Hermus River flowed into the Aegean Sea, Smyrna was one of the oldest cities in the district. Today it is known as Izmir, Turkey. After Ephesus, Smyrna was the most significant of the seven cities to whom John addressed messages in Revelation 2–3.

After Smyrna came under Roman control, its citizens were eager to demonstrate their allegiance. Smyrna fully embraced emperor worship and its authorities dealt harsh punishment to anyone refusing to participate. Jews were exempt from emperor worship, according to Roman law. However, Jewish Christians were not recognized as Jews, leaving the church in Smyrna vulnerable to persecution.

In the message to the church at Smyrna, believers were urged to stand firm in the midst of their suffering and maintain their faithfulness. They were reminded of the reward that awaits all faithful followers of Christ.

Ruins in Smyrna

SMYRNA IN THE BIBLE

This is what you must write to the angel of the church in Smyrna:

I am the first and the last. I died, but now I am alive! Listen to what I say.

I know how much you suffer and how poor you are, but you are rich. I also know the cruel things being said about you by people who claim to be God's people. But they are not really God's people. They are a group that belongs to Satan.

Don't worry about what you will suffer. The devil will throw some of you into jail, and you will be tested and made to suffer for ten days. But if you are faithful until you die, I will reward you with a glorious life.

If you have ears, listen to what the Spirit says to the churches. Whoever wins the victory will not be hurt by the second death. (Revelation 2:8–11)

■ *Polycarp (AD 69–155), one of the most famous Christian martyrs of the early church, served as the bishop of Smyrna.*

SMYRNA

Acropolis cistern
© BiblePlaces.com

During his years in Ephesus, the apostle Paul preached in the lecture hall of Tyrannus "until every Jew and Gentile in Asia had heard the Lord's message." This account in Acts 19:8–10 hints that the church in Smyrna may have been established during Paul's third missionary journey due to the proximity of Smyrna to Ephesus on the Aegean coast.

© BiblePlaces.com

PERGAMUM IN THE BIBLE

This is what you must write to the angel of the church in Pergamum:

I am the one who has the sharp double-edged sword! Listen to what I say.

I know you live where Satan has his throne. But you have kept true to my name. Right there where Satan lives, my faithful witness Antipas was taken from you and put to death. Even then you did not give up your faith in me.

I do have a few things against you. Some of you are following the teaching of Balaam. Long ago he told Balak to teach the people of Israel to eat food that had been offered to idols and to be immoral. Now some of you are following the teaching of the Nicolaitans. Turn back! If you don't, I will come quickly and fight against these people. And my words will cut like a sword.

If you have ears, listen to what the Spirit says to the churches. To everyone who wins the victory, I will give some of the hidden food. I will also give each one a white stone with a new name written on it. No one will know that name except the one who is given the stone.

(Revelation 2:12–17)

Pergamum

REVELATION 2:12–17

Pergamum is the northernmost of the churches in Asia Minor to whom the book of Revelation was addressed. The city was located about ten miles inland from the Aegean Sea and fifty miles north of Smyrna. Pergamum is identified with the modern-day city of Bergama, Turkey.

The city was known for its beauty and its impenetrable defenses. Its public buildings—which included the second-largest library in the ancient world—were built on terraces on a steep mountainside, about 1,000 feet above the surrounding valley. For centuries, Pergamum's kings controlled the major trade route from Persia to the Mediterranean.

Pergamum was known also as a center of emperor worship. Many Roman citizens believed the emperor to be a divine being. Travelers from far and wide came to Pergamum to worship at the local temple.

Since Pergamum was recognized as a difficult place for Christians to thrive because of its pervasive emperor cult, John was instructed to write these words: *"I know you live where Satan has his throne"* (Revelation 2:13). Those who refused to worship the emperor could face persecution and even death. Yet John urged believers in Pergamum to press on—to stand firm against persecution and false teaching.

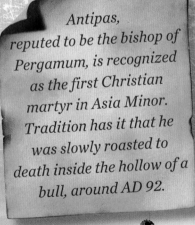

Antipas, reputed to be the bishop of Pergamum, is recognized as the first Christian martyr in Asia Minor. Tradition has it that he was slowly roasted to death inside the hollow of a bull, around AD 92.

PERGAMUM

© BiblePlaces.com

135

Thyatira

REVELATION 2:18–29

Thyatira was located in the Lycus River Valley, approximately forty miles east of the Aegean Sea in west-central Asia Minor. The city was thirty-seven miles southeast of Pergamum, thirty-seven miles northwest of Sardis, and forty-seven miles northwest of Smyrna. Today the city of Akhisar, Turkey, stands on the site. Despite the fact that three major roads ran through the city, Thyatira had very little prominence in the region.

As a result, the church in Thyatira was arguably the least significant of the seven John addressed; yet it received John's longest letter. The church was strong and faithful, but it faced a problem that threatened to tear it apart. A woman in the church, referred to as "Jezebel," was urging other Christians to tolerate the sinful practices of idol worshipers. She wanted the church to compromise its values in order to maintain its standing in the community.

Those who followed her were reminded about the dire consequences of compromise where sin is concerned. Believers in Thyatira were urged to hold fast to the truth they had been given by God.

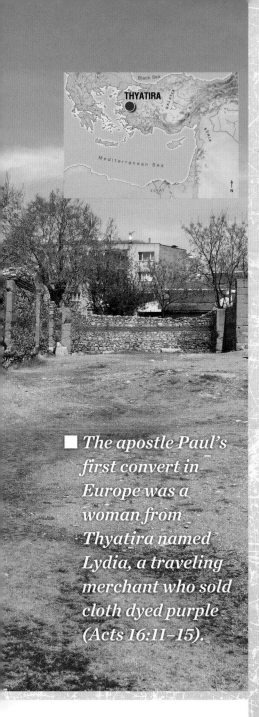

■ The apostle Paul's first convert in Europe was a woman from Thyatira named Lydia, a traveling merchant who sold cloth dyed purple (Acts 16:11–15).

THYATIRA IN THE BIBLE

This is what you must write to the angel of the church in Thyatira:

I am the Son of God! My eyes are like flames of fire, and my feet are like bronze. Listen to what I say.

I know everything about you, including your love, your faith, your service, and how you have endured. I know you are doing more now than you have ever done before. But I still have something against you because of that woman Jezebel. She calls herself a prophet, and you let her teach and mislead my servants to do immoral things and to eat food offered to idols. I gave her a chance to turn from her sins, but she did not want to stop doing these immoral things.

I am going to strike down Jezebel. Everyone who does these immoral things with her will also be punished, if they don't stop. I will even kill her followers. Then all the churches will see that I know everyone's thoughts and feelings. I will treat each of you as you deserve.

Some of you in Thyatira don't follow Jezebel's teaching. You don't know anything about what her followers call the "deep secrets of Satan." So I won't burden you down with any other commands. But until I come, you must hold firmly to the teaching you have.

I will give power over the nations to everyone who wins the victory and keeps on obeying me until the end. I will give each of them the same power my Father has given me. They will rule the nations with an iron rod and smash those nations to pieces like clay pots. I will also give them the morning star. If you have ears, listen to what the Spirit says to the churches. (Revelation 2:18–29)

"Jezebel," John's derogatory nickname for the woman in Thyatira whose false teachings were threatening the spiritual health of the church, is a reference to the wife of King Ahab. Ahab ruled over the northern kingdom of Israel in the ninth century BC. Jezebel, his wife, encouraged the Israelites to worship the Phoenician god Baal. She also tried to kill the prophet Elijah.
(For more information on Jezebel's evil life, see 1 Kings 16:29—22:40; 2 Kings 9:30–37.)

Old ruins of Artemis temple in Sardis, Turkey

SARDIS

Temple with mosaic on floor in Sardis, Turkey

According to Obadiah 20, many Jewish people who were exiled from their homeland settled in Sepharad. Scholars believe Sepharad is the Semitic name for Sardis. The ruins of a large synagogue are visible to this day in Sardis.

■ *According to the Greek historian Herodotus, the Lydians were the first people to use coins as currency, sometime between 650 and 600 BC.*

Sardis

REVELATION 3:1–6

Sardis was the capital of the Lydia region of Asia Minor. Located in the Hermus River Valley, the city lay forty-six miles east of Smyrna, twenty-eight miles west of Philadelphia, and thirty-one miles south of Thyatira. Today the city of Sart, Turkey, occupies the site.

Sardis and the entire region of Lydia were legendary for their wealth. The expression "rich as Croesus," which is used to describe a very wealthy person, derives from there. Croesus was the last king of Lydia before the region was conquered by the Persians in the sixth century BC.

After Sardis was destroyed by a massive earthquake in AD 17, the Roman emperor Tiberius helped rebuild it. The citizens of Sardis were so grateful that they made sure the emperor cult flourished in their city.

In the letter to the church in Sardis, the believers were chided for being spiritually dead and were accused of only going through the motions when it came to their commitment to God. They were warned of the dangers of becoming complacent in the Christian faith.

SARDIS IN THE BIBLE

This is what you must write to the angel of the church in Sardis:

I have the seven spirits of God and the seven stars. Listen to what I say.

I know what you are doing. Everyone may think you are alive, but you are dead. Wake up! You have only a little strength left, and it is almost gone. So try to become stronger. I have found that you are not completely obeying God. Remember the teaching you were given and heard. Hold firmly to it and turn from your sins. If you don't wake up, I will come when you least expect it, just as a thief does.

A few of you in Sardis have not dirtied your clothes with sin. You will walk with me in white clothes, because you are worthy. Everyone who wins the victory will wear white clothes. Their names will not be erased from the book of life, and I will tell my Father and his angels that they are my followers. If you have ears, listen to what the Spirit says to the churches. (Revelation 3:1–6)

Philadelphia

REVELATION 3:7–13

The ancient city of Philadelphia was located in the Lydia region of Asia Minor, approximately seventy-three miles east of Smyrna, twenty-eight miles west-southwest of Sardis, and forty-seven miles northwest of Laodicea. The city was built on a low hill at the foot of Mount Tmolas. It served as the gateway to a pass through the mountains through which all east-west commerce in the region had to pass. The town of Alaşehir, Turkey, occupies the site today.

The fertile plains of the region were ideal for agriculture—specifically, grape production. Not surprisingly, Philadelphia became a center for worship of Dionysus, the god of wine and fertility.

Despite that, the Christian church in Philadelphia was commended for its faithfulness. But harsh words were directed to the local Jewish community, which had told the local Roman officials that Jewish Christians were not true Jews. They were against anyone who followed Jesus as the Messiah.

That kind of slander was potentially life threatening for Jesus' followers. Jewish people were exempt from emperor worship. Jewish Christians, however, were not exempt, which left them vulnerable to persecution if they did not worship the emperor. The church in Philadelphia was encouraged to remain faithful to God in the midst of suffering and persecution.

The name Philadelphia, which means "brotherly love," commemorates the relationship between Attalus II Philadelphus, the king of Pergamum, and his brother and successor Eumenes II.

■ *Philadelphia was the most recently founded of the seven churches addressed by John in Revelation 2–3.*

Acropolis architrave fragment
© BiblePlaces.com

PHILADELPHIA IN THE BIBLE

This is what you must write to the angel of the church in Philadelphia:

I am the one who is holy and true, and I have the keys that belonged to David. When I open a door, no one can close it. And when I close a door, no one can open it. Listen to what I say.

I know everything you have done. And I have placed before you an open door no one can close. You were not very strong, but you obeyed my message and did not deny you are my followers. Now you will see what I will do with those people who belong to Satan's group. They claim to be God's people, but they are liars. I will make them come and kneel down at your feet. Then they will know that I love you.

You obeyed my message and endured. So I will protect you from the time of testing everyone in all the world must go through. I am coming soon. So hold firmly to what you have, and no one will take away the crown that you will be given as your reward.

Everyone who wins the victory will be made into a pillar in the temple of my God, and they will stay there forever. I will write on each of them the name of my God and the name of his city. It is the new Jerusalem my God will send down from heaven. I will also write on them my own new name. If you have ears, listen to what the Spirit says to the churches. (Revelation 3:7–13)

Snow-covered mountain west of Philadelphia
© BiblePlaces.com

141

LAODICEA IN THE BIBLE

This is what you must write to the angel of the church in Laodicea:

I am the one called Amen! I am the faithful and true witness and the source of God's creation. Listen to what I say.

I know everything you have done, and you are not cold or hot. I wish you were either one or the other. But since you are lukewarm and neither cold nor hot, I will spit you out of my mouth. You claim to be rich and successful and to have everything you need. But you don't know how bad off you are. You are pitiful, poor, blind, and naked.

Buy your gold from me. It has been refined in a fire, and it will make you rich. Buy white clothes from me. Wear them and you can cover up your shameful nakedness. Buy medicine for your eyes, so you will be able to see.

I correct and punish everyone I love. So make up your minds to turn away from your sins. Listen! I am standing and knocking at your door. If you hear my voice and open the door, I will come in and we will eat together. Everyone who wins the victory will sit with me on my throne, just as I won the victory and sat with my Father on his throne. If you have ears, listen to what the Spirit says to the churches. (Revelation 3:14–22)

Laodicea

REVELATION 3:14–22

Built on a plateau in the Phrygia region of Asia Minor, Laodicea was located approximately one hundred miles east of Ephesus and forty-five miles southeast of Philadelphia—near modern-day Denizli, Turkey. The city was built at the intersection of a major north-south road that ran from Pergamum to the Mediterranean Sea and an east-west road that ran from Ephesus to the interior of Asia Minor.

S uch favorable geography allowed Laodicea to become an important commercial city in the Roman Empire. The city was known for its financial wealth, its vast textile industry, and a medicinal eye salve produced there. (John touched on all three in Revelation 3:18.)

In the third century BC, the Seleucid king Antiochus the Great resettled 2,000 Jewish families from Babylon in the Laodicean region. From that time, the local Jewish population grew steadily. In the first century AD, that population—specifically, Jewish converts to Christianity—helped establish the church in Laodicea as one of the most important congregations in the region.

The people of Laodicea were likely introduced to Christianity during the apostle Paul's third missionary journey. Though Paul did not visit Laodicea himself, he spent close to three years in Ephesus. News of his teachings likely spread from there throughout Asia Minor. A believer from nearby Colossae named Epaphras is credited with founding the church in Laodicea.

By the time John wrote to the church in Laodicea, it was a mere shell of its former self. It stood alone among the seven churches as the only one about which nothing good was said. Like the people of Laodicea, the church had become complacent and self-satisfied.

■ *The apostle Paul mentioned the believers in Laodicea in his letter to the church in Colossae (Colossians 2:1). He intended for the letter to the Colossians to be read in the church of Laodicea as well. Laodicea was about eleven miles from Colossae.*

In his letter to the Colossian church, Paul referred to a letter he sent to the Laodicean church (Colossians 4:16). Some scholars believe this letter originally accompanied three other letters from Paul—Ephesians, Colossians, and Philemon—but was subsequently lost. Others believe Paul was actually referring to Ephesians, which may have originally been intended for the Laodiceans.

143

Introduction

The spread of the gospel to Greece was part of the fourth wave of evangelism in the wake of Jesus' resurrection and ascension. The first wave was limited to the regions of Galilee, Samaria, and Judea—places where Jesus had personally ministered. The second wave extended northward—into Tyre, across the Mediterranean (including the island of Cyprus), and all the way to Tarsus. The third wave, marked by the apostle Paul's first missionary journey in AD 48, carried the good news about Jesus into Asia Minor.

The fourth wave marked a radical turning point in first-century Christian evangelism. When Paul took the gospel to Greece during his second and third missionary journeys, he spent a good part of

his time talking to Gentiles—that is, non-Jewish people. No longer would the good news of Christ be delivered mainly to Jewish communities.

The people of Greece proved very receptive to the gospel message. The Christian communities that sprung up in Corinth, Philippi, Thessalonica, and Antioch held a dear place in Paul's heart for the rest of his life.

The specter of Rome loomed large over Christianity in the first century AD. As the seat of power in an empire that spanned three continents, Rome dictated the way millions of people lived and worshiped. Initially, Rome regarded Christianity with varying levels of

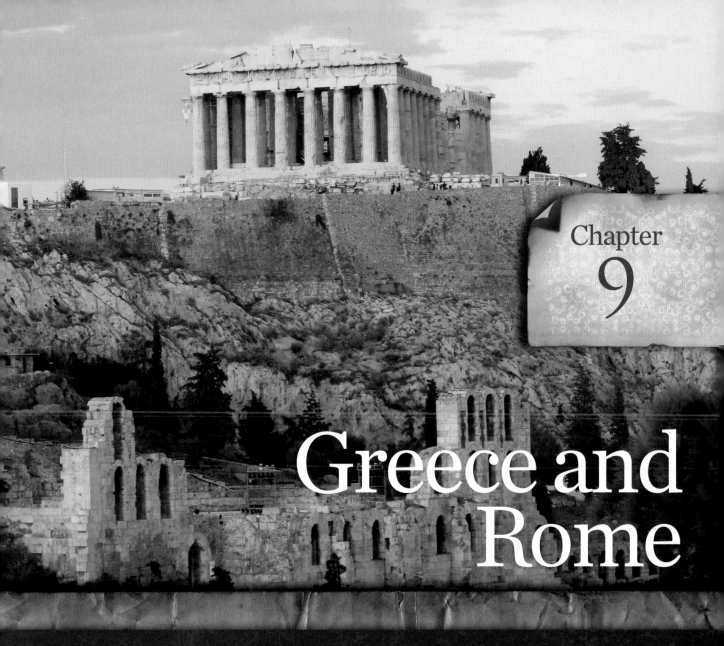

Greece and Rome

disinterest. As far as Rome was concerned, Christianity was nothing more than a minor offshoot of Judaism.

However, three factors eventually changed Rome's perspective. The first was constant complaining from Jewish leaders who demanded that Rome take action against what they regarded as a blasphemous sect. In AD 49, Emperor Claudius temporarily expelled all Jews and Christians from Rome because of the tumult (Acts 18:2).

The second factor was the explosive growth of the Christian movement. In twenty short years, Christianity gained footholds throughout Palestine, Asia Minor, and Greece. Its growth

coincided—and competed—with the rise of emperor worship in the Roman world.

A third factor that changed the empire's stance toward Christianity was a fire that devastated Rome in AD 64. Looking for scapegoats to deflect attention away from himself, Emperor Nero blamed Christians for the citywide blaze. Thus began an era of Christian persecution that continued sporadically for the next three centuries. Both Peter and Paul were put to death in Rome.

In AD 313, Emperor Constantine I issued the Edict of Milan, which effectively put an end to Christian persecution in Rome. Less than seventy years later, in 380, Christianity was named the official religion of the Roman Empire.

Corinth

1 AND 2 CORINTHIANS

The city of Corinth was built on the narrowest section of the isthmus that connects mainland Greece with its southern peninsula—the Peloponnese. Located at the base of an 1,800-foot monolithic rock, Corinth boasted a virtually impregnable acropolis known as the Acrocorinth.

Few cities in the ancient world were more ideally situated for commerce. All overland trade from Greece to the Peloponnese passed through Corinth. In addition, the city maintained ports on both sides of the isthmus—Lechaio (or Lechaion, its ancient name) on the Corinth Gulf and Cenchreae on the Saronic Gulf. Not only was the city eminently accessible from any direction but it also controlled the seas on both sides of Greece. Corinth also featured a five-foot-wide track for wheeling ships across the isthmus, thus eliminating the need to sail around the southern peninsula.

Corinth was founded in the tenth century BC by Dorian Greeks. As the city grew, its people fortified its stronghold and its influence in the region. During the Peloponnesian War (431–404 BC), Corinth sided with Sparta, which triumphed over Athens. Scholars estimate the city's population at that time was around 100,000.

In 243 BC, Corinth became part of the Achaean League, a confederation of Greek city-states that ultimately gained control of the Peloponnese. Corinth was the leader of the league when Rome demanded that it be dissolved in 147 BC. The league revolted against Rome, which led to Corinth's utter destruction when Roman forces led by Lucius Mummius razed the city.

One hundred years later, Julius Caesar rebuilt Corinth and populated it with Italian freedmen. Greeks from neighboring areas joined them, giving the city a distinctly cosmopolitan flavor. Public inscriptions were in Latin, yet most of the population spoke Greek. In 27 BC, Corinth was named capital of the Roman province of Achaia.

The Bible first mentions Corinth in Acts 18, in conjunction with the apostle Paul's second missionary journey. Paul arrived in Corinth around AD 52. There he met a Christian couple—Aquila and Priscilla—who worked as tent makers. A tent maker himself, Paul stayed and worked alongside them.

Ruins of the Temple of Apollo in ancient Corinth

Ruins in Corinth

CORINTH

According to Acts 20:2–3, during Paul's third missionary journey, he traveled to Greece and stayed there for three months. Scholars believe he spent most of this time in Corinth. Some suggest it was from there that he wrote his letter to the church in Rome—that is, the New Testament book of Romans.

Corinth was home to the Temple of Aphrodite, which may have employed up to 1,000 prostitutes as part of it worship, leading to Corinth's reputation for sexual promiscuity. So pervasive was Corinth's reputation for sexual deviance that Aristophanes coined the word *corinthianize*, which means "to practice immorality."

Tetrapylon Gate in Aphrodisias

Every Sabbath, Paul taught and debated in the local Jewish synagogue, trying to persuade Jews and Greeks to embrace the truth about Jesus. The Jewish leaders in Corinth opposed Paul vehemently. Undaunted, he took his message to the Corinthian Gentiles, who proved much more receptive.

One night the Lord spoke to Paul in a dream, encouraging him to continue his ministry despite intense opposition (Acts 18:9–10). Paul stayed in Corinth for a year and a half, teaching believers and sharing the good news with everyone he could. He left Corinth around AD 53, along with Aquila and Priscilla. The believers he left behind, though, were never far from Paul's mind.

In the spring of AD 56, while Paul was in Ephesus, he received word that factions had developed in the church at Corinth. Other reports suggested that the Corinthian believers were struggling with immorality. Moved to take action, Paul wrote a letter to them in which he praised them for their spiritual gifts and confronted their immaturity. He addressed areas of weakness—divisions, disloyalty, moral lapses—and offered advice for dealing with each. He cleared up misunderstandings about the Lord's Supper and Jesus' resurrection. Finally he urged the Corinthian church members to send aid to poverty-stricken believers in Jerusalem. This letter is the New Testament book of 1 Corinthians.

Paul later wrote a second letter to the believers in Corinth—this time from Macedonia. The Corinthian church had been infiltrated by false teachers who questioned Paul's integrity. At issue was the fact that Paul had planned to pay two quick visits to Corinth but ended up paying one long visit instead. The false teachers said this was proof that Paul could not be trusted. They claimed he was not a genuine apostle and accused him of lining his own pockets with the money the church had sent to help the needy believers in Jerusalem. In his letter, Paul defended himself against these charges and assured the Corinthians that he was coming to them soon. This letter is the New Testament book of 2 Corinthians.

Corinth remains a popular destination for Christian pilgrims—not only for its significance in church history, but also for its well-preserved ruins. Archaeologists have excavated rows of shops like the one Paul worked in with Aquila and Priscilla. They have uncovered villas that help us understand the environment in which first-century "house churches" met.

CORINTH
IN THE BIBLE

From Paul, chosen by God to be an apostle of Christ Jesus, and from Sosthenes, who is also a follower.
To God's church in Corinth. Christ Jesus chose you to be his very own people, and you worship in his name, as we and all others do who call him Lord.
(1 Corinthians 1:1–2)

Philippi

PHILIPPIANS

Philippi was an ancient city in eastern Macedonia, ten miles inland from the Aegean Sea. Surrounded on three sides by mountains, the city boasted an impressive acropolis. In 42 BC, the Roman general Mark Antony settled many veterans from his army in the city and established Philippi as a Roman colony.

The city enters the New Testament narrative as part of a vision the apostle Paul received while he was in Troas during his second missionary journey (around AD 50). In the vision, a Macedonian man begged Paul to come and help people there. Paul left immediately for Philippi (Acts 16:9–12). During his visit, he established a church in the city—his first in Europe.

The church in Philippi held a special place in the apostle's heart for years to come, as evidenced by the warm language he used in his letter to the believers there. Paul returned to Philippi more than once during his missionary journeys.

Philippi archaeological site

Archaeological area of ancient Philippi

PHILIPPI IN THE BIBLE

My friends at Philippi, you remember what it was like when I started preaching the good news in Macedonia. After I left there, you were the only church that became my partner by giving blessings and by receiving them in return. (Philippians 4:15)

Thessalonica

1 AND 2 THESSALONIANS

The Macedonian city of Thessalonica was located at the head of the Thermaic Gulf. Two major Roman roads intersected in the city, making it an important center for communication and commerce.

The Church of the Rotonda in **Thessalonica**

According to Acts 17:1–13, the apostle Paul visited Thessalonica during his second missionary journey. He was accompanied by Silas. As was his custom, Paul went to the synagogue on the Sabbath to proclaim the good news about Jesus.

A number of Jews, Gentiles, and prominent women in the community responded positively to Paul's message. They formed the nucleus of the Thessalonian church. However, this overwhelming response did not sit well with other Jews in the city. They recruited local rabble-rousers to start a riot, and Paul and Silas were forced to flee.

Nevertheless, the growth of the Thessalonian church could not be stopped. Paul continued to teach, reprimand, encourage, and inspire believers in Thessalonica through his letters, the New Testament books known as 1 and 2 Thessalonians.

THESSALONICA IN THE BIBLE

From Paul, Silas, and Timothy. To the church in Thessalonica, the people of God the Father and of the Lord Jesus Christ. I pray that God will be kind to you and will bless you with peace! (1 Thessalonians 1:1)

Paul's Words to the Church in Thessalonica

1 THESSALONIANS 1:1–10

From Paul, Silas, and Timothy.

To the church in Thessalonica, the people of God the Father and of the Lord Jesus Christ.

I pray that God will be kind to you and will bless you with peace!

We thank God for you and always mention you in our prayers. Each time we pray, we tell God our Father about your faith and loving work and about your firm hope in our Lord Jesus Christ.

My dear friends, God loves you, and we know he has chosen you to be his people. When we told you the good news, it was with the power and assurance that come from the Holy Spirit, and not simply with words. You knew what kind of people we were and how we helped you. So, when you accepted the message, you followed our example and the example of the Lord. You suffered, but the Holy Spirit made you glad.

You became an example for all the Lord's followers in Macedonia and Achaia. And because of you, the Lord's message has spread everywhere in those regions. Now the news of your faith in God is known all over the world, and we don't have to say a thing about it. Everyone is talking about how you welcomed us and how you turned away from idols to serve the true and living God. They also tell how you are waiting for his Son Jesus to come from heaven. God raised him from death, and on the day of judgment Jesus will save us from God's anger.

Athens

ACTS 17:16–34

After being driven from Thessalonica and Berea during his second missionary journey, Paul retreated to the relatively safer environment of Athens. While waiting for his traveling companions to join him, Paul spent time taking in the city and its impressive architecture: the Acropolis, the Parthenon, the Erechtheion, the Temple of Hephaestus, and more.

Everywhere he looked, Paul saw idols. Athens was teeming with temples and shrines. As he did in almost every city he visited, Paul headed for the synagogue, where he engaged local Jews and God-fearing Greeks in a discussion about false gods versus the real God.

Intrigued by his message, a group of philosophers invited Paul to a meeting at the Areopagus, where learned Athenians debated the merits of new philosophies and religions. Paul addressed the assembly, but the response was underwhelming. A few people put their faith in Christ; the rest regarded Paul's faith as a mere curiosity.

View of the Acropolis at sunset, Athens, Greece

Ancient theater under the Acropolis

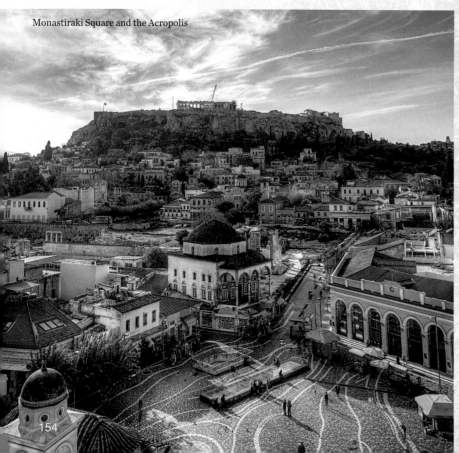

Monastiraki Square and the Acropolis

ATHENS
IN THE BIBLE

While Paul was waiting in Athens, he was upset to see all the idols in the city. (Acts 17:16)

Colosseum in Rome, Italy

Rome

ROMANS

The city of Rome served as the seat of power for one of the greatest empires the world has ever known. Built on and around seven hills in eastern Italy, the city was known for its stunning advances in architecture and public works. Roman architects were responsible for such memorable structures as the Circus Maximus, the Colosseum, and Trajan's Column.

Though its place in world history looms large, Rome plays a small but pivotal role in the New Testament narrative. Little is known about how or when Christianity came to the city. By the time the apostle Paul wrote his letter to the believers in Rome—the letter we know as the New Testament book of Romans—the church there was already well established and respected (Romans 1:7–8).

Paul wrote his letter to the Romans before he had even visited the church. As a result, he did not address personal matters, as he did in many of his other letters. Instead, Paul focused on the heart of the gospel. He talked about sin, salvation, grace, righteousness, death, and resurrection. Paul hoped to take this gospel to the farthest reaches of the Roman Empire, and he hoped to make the Roman church his base of support.

A few years later, around AD 60, Paul arrived in Rome to stand trial for charges stemming from a confrontation he'd had with some Jews from Roman Asia several years earlier. Paul was placed under house arrest in Rome for two years, during which time he met with church leaders and continued to share the good news about Jesus every chance he got.

This is where the biblical narrative of Paul ends. Tradition holds that Paul was beheaded in Rome during the reign of Nero and that Peter, who was not a Roman citizen, was crucified upside down during the same period.

Scaled model of ancient Rome

ROME IN THE BIBLE

This letter is to all of you in Rome. God loves you and has chosen you to be his very own people. I pray that God our Father and our Lord Jesus Christ will be kind to you and will bless you with peace! (Romans 1:7)

Paul requested to stand trial in Rome rather than be sent back to Jerusalem, where attempts already had been made on his life. Paul exercised his right as a Roman citizen to appeal his case to the emperor (Acts 25:1–12).

Basilica of Saint Paul Outside the Walls

According to Christian tradition, the apostle Paul was executed in Rome around AD 64, as part of the persecution that took place during the reign of Nero. Paul's body was buried in a nearby tomb, which was marked with a memorial.

In the third century AD, the Roman emperor Constantine ordered the construction of a basilica over the site. In 386, Emperor Theodosius I began work on a much grander and more ornate structure. Thus began centuries of building and rebuilding the Basilica of Saint Paul.

Gregory the Great (590–604) oversaw extensive modifications of the church, including the placement of an altar directly over Paul's tomb. The basilica was damaged during the Saracen invasion of Rome in the ninth century. Pope John VIII oversaw its repair and fortification.

In 1823 a fire caused by a negligent worker repairing the roof nearly destroyed the church. Mosaics on the triumphal arch of the structure were some of the only original elements to survive. The basilica reopened in 1840 and was reconsecrated by Pope Pius IX in 1855.

The builders maintained the original design of the structure, with one nave and four aisles. Eighty columns line the nave on both sides. The entire structure is now 420 feet long, 210 feet wide, and 100 feet tall. After an explosion destroyed the church's windows in 1891, their glass was replaced with alabaster.

Millions of Christians have made the pilgrimage to Rome to pay tribute to the apostle Paul and to admire the basilica that bears his name.

The Basilica of Saint Paul is the second-largest church in Rome. Saint Peter's Basilica is the largest.

Saint Paul's Outside the Walls is one of four papal basilicas. The other three are Saint John Lateran, Saint Mary Major, and Saint Peter's (see pages 160-161).

SAINT PAUL IN THE BIBLE

When the crowd heard Paul speak to them in Aramaic, they became even quieter. Then Paul said: "I am a Jew, born in the city of Tarsus in Cilicia. But I grew up here in Jerusalem where I was a student of Gamaliel and was taught to follow every single law of our ancestors. In fact, I was just as eager to obey God as any of you are today." (Acts 22:2–3)

Basilica of Saint Paul Outside the Walls

Saint Peter's Basilica

Christian tradition holds that the apostle Peter was put to death in Rome during the reign of Nero, around AD 64. Peter's body was buried just outside the Circus of Nero in a grave marked by a red rock. Years later a shrine was built on the spot.

The third-century theologian Origen reported that Peter was sentenced to crucifixion. Because Peter declared himself unworthy to be put to death in the same manner as Jesus, he requested that he be crucified upside down.

Sometime between AD 319 and 333, Emperor Constantine oversaw the construction of a basilica on the site. The church, known today as Old Saint Peter's Basilica, was constructed in the traditional Latin Cross style and was over 340 feet long. It was an impressive structure, but eventually it fell into disrepair.

More than a thousand years later, Pope Nicholas V asked the Italian architect Bernardo Rossellino to design an entirely new basilica. Nicholas's successor, Pope Julius II, had a grander vision for the basilica and chose an architectural design submitted by Donato Bramante instead. The cornerstone was laid in 1506.

Over the next 120 years, a succession of popes and architects oversaw the construction of the new Saint Peter's Basilica. At one point, Michelangelo himself was brought in to give cohesion to the variety of designs and ideas.

The results are stunning. Cruciform in shape, the basilica's central space houses one of the largest domes in the world. Individual chapels, each uniquely designed and ornately appointed, surround the dome and line the wide aisles that frame the nave. Some of the world's great art and sculptures can be found inside the basilica. The entire structure covers just under six acres.

Saint Peter's Basilica is the pinnacle of Renaissance architecture. Its central dome dominates the skyline of Rome. Millions of Christians making the pilgrimage to Rome to worship God stand in awe of perhaps one of the largest churches in all Christendom.

SAINT PETER
IN THE BIBLE

Jesus told him: "Simon, son of Jonah, you are blessed! You didn't discover this on your own. It was shown to you by my Father in heaven. So I will call you Peter, which means 'a rock.' On this rock I will build my church, and death itself will not have any power over it. I will give you the keys to the kingdom of heaven, and God in heaven will allow whatever you allow on earth. But he will not allow anything you don't allow."

(Matthew 16:17–19)

Inside St. Peter's Basilica, Vatican

Introduction

The New Testament story ends with the good news about Jesus having reached Rome and its surrounding areas. The era of Roman persecution had dawned, and the nascent church was facing an extinction-level threat.

The gospel, however, could not be contained. Nor could God's people be silenced. The good news spilled over Italy's borders in all directions. Intrepid missionaries carried the message of Jesus throughout Europe and beyond, heedless of their own safety. Many paid the ultimate price, sacrificing their lives for their faith.

AD 313 marked a seismic shift in church history. That year, the Roman emperor Constantine issued the Edict of Milan, legalizing Christian worship. Thus began a fertile era for evangelization—and a golden age for church construction. Constantine's mother, Helena, spearheaded the effort. She traveled to the Holy Land to identify its sacred locations and to oversee the construction of shrines and monuments on these sites. Many of these monuments were later replaced by bigger, grander, and more impressive structures—some of which are still standing today.

Around the World

In the seventeen centuries that followed, the gospel worked its way to every corner of the globe. In its wake it has left some of the most impressive and inspiring structures ever built—to say nothing of billions of changed lives. In this final chapter, we will look at eight of these structures.

These churches represent a wide array of
- chronological eras
- geographical regions
- architectural styles
- backgrounds and histories
- spiritual perspectives

What they share is a common foundation—the promise of Jesus in Matthew 18:20:

"Whenever two or three of you come together in my name, I am there with you."

Mont-Saint-Michel Abbey

ont-Saint-Michel is a rocky island a half mile off the northwestern coast of France. The island is almost 250 acres in size and is connected to the mainland by a causeway that was built in 1878.

Once a Gallo-Roman stronghold, Mont-Saint-Michel became home to a monastery originally established in the eighth century. Tradition states that the location for this abbey was inspired by Saint Aubert (bishop of Avranches). He claimed to have seen a vision in AD 708 of the archangel Michael, who instructed him to build a church at this site.

After the French Revolution, the abbey was converted to a prison for political prisoners, which drew the opposition of many, including well-known author Victor Hugo. The prison closed in 1863, and by 1874 the island was declared a national, historic monument. The abbey was reopened in 1969 and remains active today. Once a remote location where monks could find solitude, Mont-Saint-Michel now receives more than three million tourists a year and contains a few hotels, retail businesses, and tourist attractions.

> "The Mont-Saint-Michel is for France what the Great Pyramid is for Egypt."
>
> VICTOR HUGO

FRANCE

The Church of Hallgrímur

REYKJAVÍC, ICELAND

Located in Iceland's capital of Reykjavík, the Church of Hallgrímur stands as a striking landmark that can be seen from almost any vantage point in the city. The lines of the 244-foot steeple drive the eye upward to heaven. In addition to the spiritual aspect of the design, the architecture resembles Iceland's mountains and volcanic basalt. This Lutheran church, built over a period of thirty years, was completed in 1974.

Notre Dame

Construction of the Notre Dame de la Chapelle (Our Lady of the Chapel) began in 1210 and continued for nearly a century. The building reflects both Romanesque and Gothic influence.

PARIS, FRANCE

LONDON,
ENGLAND

Westminster Abbey

Westminster Abbey, also called the Collegiate Church of Saint Peter at Westminster, is perhaps best known as the traditional site where British monarchs are crowned and where many have been buried.

According to tradition, a church was first built on this site in the seventh century AD, after a fisherman on the Thames River reported seeing a vision of the apostle Peter.

In the mid-eleventh century, King Edward the Confessor began an extensive reconstruction of the church, known as Saint Peter's Abbey, in order to make a proper royal burial site. Edward died in 1065, approximately twenty-five years before the reconstruction was completed. He became the first king buried in the church. A year later, William the Conqueror was the first-known monarch to be crowned in the Abbey.

In 1245, King Henry III, a spiritual heir of Edward the Confessor, ordered the Abbey rebuilt in Anglo-French Gothic style. Like Edward, Henry wanted a church fit for his own burial. Work on the Abbey continued until 1517, resulting in the structure that exists today. Two western towers were added in the early eighteenth century.

Las Lajas Cathedral

In 1754, Maria Mueces and her daughter Rosa, who was deaf and mute, got caught in a lightning storm and took refuge in a nearby gorge. According to Roman Catholic tradition, Maria's daughter saw an image of the Virgin Mary silhouetted on a cliff face above the river— at which point Rosa spoke for the first time in her life.

To commemorate the miraculous event, locals built a shrine made of straw and wood. In 1802, a larger shrine was constructed, along with a bridge that extended to the opposite side of the canyon, over the Guáitara River.

Construction of the current church began in 1916 and continued for thirty-three years. The neo-Gothic structure rises over three hundred feet from the canyon floor and connects with a bridge that makes it accessible from either side of the gorge. The cliff face on which the Virgin Mary's image appears also serves as the back wall of the church.

COLOMBIA

Hagia Sophia

Hagia Sophia's paradise-like beauty and Byzantine architectural brilliance has influenced the Eastern Orthodox, Roman Catholic, and Muslim world alike. Before the city was named Istanbul, it was known as Constantinople.

Originally called the Megale Ekklesia, or the "Great Church," Hagia Sophia (which means "Holy Wisdom") has always been among the grandest places of worship. The first structure was dedicated in 360 by Emperor Constantius, son of Emperor Constantine, the city's founder. Riots in 404 and 532 destroyed the masterpiece twice, prompting Emperor Justinian I in 532 to order the church be rebuilt to its former splendor. After it was completed in 537, the building's impressive beauty moved Justinian to remark, "Solomon, I have outdone thee!" Thus, Hagia Sophia has also been called a "second Jerusalem."

In 1204 the cathedral was attacked, desecrated, and plundered by the Crusaders, solidifying the separation of the Greek Orthodox and Roman Catholic churches. From 537 – 1453 it served as the seat of the Patriarchate of Constantinople. In 1453 the Islamic conqueror Sultan Mehmet II turned the church into a mosque, and in 1934 it was converted into a museum by the Republic of Turkey.

DRESDEN, GERMANY

The Frauenkirche

The Church of Our Lady (also known as the Dresden Frauenkirche) was built between 1726 and 1743. Its design reflected the Protestant influences of the times. Architect George Bähr placed the altar, pulpit, and baptismal font directly centered from the perspective of the congregation. The church featured one of the largest domes in Europe.

The Frauenkirche stood for three hundred years, until the closing days of World War II, when it was destroyed during the bombing of Dresden in 1945. German leaders opted to leave the remains intact as an anti-war memorial.

Reconstruction began in 1993. The church's original materials, which had been carefully numbered and cataloged after the war, figured prominently in the rebuilding effort. The reconstruction was completed in 2005. Today the church serves as a symbol of reconciliation between former enemies.

Saint Basil's Cathedral

L ocated in the geometric center of Moscow—in Red Square—this Russian Orthodox church (also known as the Cathedral of the Protection of Most Holy Theotokos on the Moat) stands as a pinnacle of Byzantine architecture.

The cathedral's design, which mimics a flame rising into the sky, was absolutely unique. No known precedents exist. The cathedral consists of eight individual churches—four large and four small—surrounding a core. The four large churches are octagonal in shape and are positioned at the four major compass headings. The four smaller, cube-shaped churches are positioned on the corners. The result is a symmetrical, unified whole.

Construction of the church began in 1555 on the orders of Ivan the Terrible. Though initial construction ended in 1561, the cathedral has been a work in progress ever since. The onion-shaped domes were given their vivid colors in stages, from the late seventeenth century to the mid-nineteenth century.

MOSCOW, RUSSIA

History and Mission of American Bible Society

Established in 1816, American Bible Society's history is closely intertwined with the history of a nation whose founding preceded its own by less than a generation. In fact, the Society's early leadership reads like a Who's Who of patriots and other notable Americans of the time. Its first president was Elias Boudinot, formerly the President of the Continental Congress. John Jay, John Quincy Adams, DeWitt Clinton, and chronicler of the new nation James Fennimore Cooper also played significant roles, as would Rutherford B. Hayes and Benjamin Harrison in later generations.

From the beginning, the Bible Society's mission was to respond to the civic and spiritual needs of a fast-growing, diverse population in a rapidly expanding nation. From the new frontier beyond the Appalachian Mountains, missionaries sent back dire reports of towns that did not have a single copy of the Bible to share among its citizens. State and local Bible Societies did not have the resources, network, or capability of filling this growing need. Only a national organization would be able to do so. Once founded, ABS committed itself to organizational and technological innovation. No longer subject to British restrictions, ABS could set up its own printing plants, develop better qualities of paper and ink, and establish a network of colporteurs to get the Bibles to the people who needed them.

Reaching out to diverse audiences has always been at the heart of ABS's mission. Scriptures were made available to Native American peoples in their own languages—in Delaware in 1818, followed soon by Mohawk, Seneca, Ojibwa, Cherokee, and others. French and Spanish Bibles were published for the Louisiana Territory, Florida, and the Southwest. By the 1890s ABS was printing or distributing Scriptures in German, Portuguese, Chinese, Italian, Russian, Danish, Polish, Hungarian, Czech, and other languages to meet the spiritual needs of an increasing immigrant population. In 1836, seventy-five years before the first Braille Bibles were produced, ABS was providing Scriptures to the blind in "raised letter" editions. Responding to the need for Bibles in the languages and formats that speak most deeply to people's hearts continues to be a priority of ABS. Through its partnerships with other national Bible Societies, ABS can provide some portion of Scripture in almost any language that has a written form. It has also been able to provide Braille Scriptures for the blind; recorded Scriptures for the visually impaired, dyslexic, and people who have not yet learned to read; as well as Bible stories in sign language for the deaf.

The Bible Society's founders and their successors have always understood the Bible as a text that can speak to people's deepest needs during in times of crisis. ABS distributed its first Scriptures to the military in 1817 when it provided New Testaments to the crew of the USS *John Adams*, a frigate that had served in the War of 1812 and was continuing its service to the country by protecting the American Coast from pirates. During the Civil War, ABS provided Testaments to both northern and southern forces, and has continued to provide Bibles and Testaments to the U.S. military forces during every subsequent war, conflict, and operation. During the painful post-Reconstruction era when Jim Crow laws prevailed in many parts of the nation, ABS was able to provide Scriptures to African Americans through its partnership with the Agency Among Colored People of the South and through the historic Black churches. This faith that the Word of God speaks in special ways during times of crisis continues to inform ABS's mission. In recent years the Bible Society has produced Scripture booklets addressing the needs of people with HIV and AIDS and for those experiencing profound loss due to acts of terrorism and natural disasters.

Translation and scholarship are key components to the Bible Society's mission of faithfully and powerfully communicating the Word of God. In the mid-twentieth century, ABS, in partnership with the United Bible Societies, developed innovative theories and practices of translation, under the leadership of Eugene A. Nida. First, they insisted that all of the Bible translations they sponsored be done exclusively by native speakers, with biblical and linguistic experts serving only as translation consultants to provide technical support and guidance. From the lively and heart-felt translations that resulted, Bible Society scholars were able to see the power of translations that were rendered not on a word-for-word basis, but on a meaning-for-meaning basis that respected the natural rhythms and idioms of the target languages. This practice of "functional equivalence" translation led to a new line of Bible translations in English and was, in part, responsible for the explosion of new translations of the Bible that came out in the past thirty years. These include the Bible Society's own *Good News Translation* and *Contemporary English Version*, as well as other non-English translations.

As an organization dedicated to preparing well-researched, faithful translations, ABS has necessarily committed itself to the pursuit of scholarly excellence. In cooperation with the United Bible Societies, ABS has helped develop and publish authoritative Greek and Hebrew texts, Handbooks on the different books of the Bible, dictionaries, and other technical aids. To provide the most up-to-date training and the broadest access to all the relevant disciplines, the Nida Institute for Biblical Scholarship offers professional development seminars and workshops, hosts symposia, and publishes a journal and monograph series, all in a effort to ensure that translators communicate the Word of God powerfully to God's people around the world. For churches and readers seeking a deeper understanding of the Bible and its background, ABS has developed study Bibles, multimedia video translations with DVD extras, Scriptures in special formats, and website resources.

For almost two centuries, ABS has maintained its commitment to innovation and excellence. While the challenges it has faced over the years have changed, the Society's mission has remained constant—*to make the Bible available to every person in a language and format each can understand and afford so all people may experience its life-changing message.*

To find out more about American Bible Society please go to www.**americanbible**.org or www.**bibles**.com.